Creative Drama
for
Senior Adults

A Program for Dynamic Living in Retirement

Isabel B. Burger

Morehouse-Barlow Co., Inc.
Wilton, Connecticut

Copyright © 1980
Morehouse-Barlow Company, Inc.
All rights reserved

ISBN 0-8192-1269-5

Library of Congress Catalog Card No. 80-81101

Printed in the United States of America

*Cover design by Daniel Sullivan. Top left
and bottom right are taken from the author's
creative drama pilot project. Both
photographs by William L. Klender. Top
right is from a production in Jolantha
Kerschnagel's creative drama workshop.
Photograph by Glen Faber. Bottom left
portrays participants in Irma Paule's creative
drama workshop. Both photographs courtesy
of Brookdale Drama Project, directed by
Milton Polsky.*

Morehouse-Barlow Company, Inc.
78 Danbury Road
Wilton, Connecticut 06897

*I dedicate this book with love
and gratitude*

TO MY SENIOR FRIENDS

*those dear people who have
brightened their lives and mine
as we have laughed, cried,
hoped, shared, and grown
together through our dynamic
creative experience.*

Acknowledgements

As I think back on my first dreams of experimenting with these techniques, many dear faces and supportive words fill precious memories. All have contributed,—all have inspired, —all must share any plaudits the text receives! This small space cannot contain the full record. There are, however, a few whose important roles I must recognize with gratitude.

First come Sister Cleophas and my old friend Margery Harriss, who urged me to introduce the idea at the first meeting of the Creative Living program for Seniors at Loyola College, in Baltimore.

To Sister Kathleen Marie, Chairman of the Drama Department at the College of Notre Dame of Maryland, a brilliant, far-sighted teacher, and a sensitive friend, my gratitude for her vision and courage. The first grant, which she secured, made the early experiments possible.

The help of Joyce Di Rienzi, my able assistant on the Notre Dame projects, was invaluable. Her creative ideas gave new life to the program.

The enthusiastic support of Mr. Timothy Fagan, Director of the Department of Aging of Baltimore County, contributed much to this text. The material used in the training program I was invited to conduct for his Senior Center leaders makes up a large part of this text.

I am ever grateful to my many friends in the American Theatre Association, especially Dr. Nellie McCaslin and Dr. C. Robert Kase who have contributed to prod me to "get it down on paper."

My thanks also go to Ms. Jacqueline Sunderland, Director of

the Center for Arts and Aging of the National Council on the Aging, for the same kind of encouragement.

To Stephanie Caffrey and the editorial staff at Morehouse-Barlow, publishers, I am deeply indebted for their trust. The acceptance of a manuscript, which is somewhat removed from their focus of interest, is patent evidence of special confidence and I am grateful.

And lastly, I lift a daily prayer of thanksgiving to my Creator, who has seen fit to extend my life energies long enough for me to share valuable experiences with others who will carry on in service.

Contents

Foreword

To my creative drama colleagues, whose work with children and young people I have deeply admired for so many years, and with whom I have happily exchanged ideas, I feel I owe an explanation. Their first question, as they open this book, is bound to be: "Has Isabel changed courses completely—has she deserted the children? I thought her focus in creative drama was always children and their teachers." And the query will be justified! I have devoted half a century to thousands of young people whom I cherish, especially for the inspiration they have given to me. No—most assuredly—I have *not* deserted the children! Even as I started the pilot project for seniors at the College of Notre Dame, I conducted a creative drama demonstration class, for ages 11 to 13, where education majors and teachers could observe and learn. Because the awakening of my interest in adapting my techniques for use with seniors happened in such a strange way, I feel compelled to share it with my readers.

An Exciting Discovery

My involvement in this project started in the spring of 1975, when I helped plan a program in "Creative Living" for seniors at Loyola College in Baltimore. Since I was asked to give the opening lecture, with no limitation on subject matter, I decided to present to my captive audience of 160 men and women my strong conviction of many years: that the creative drama experience can be instrumental in effecting refreshment, renewal, and self-confidence in the mature adult. The result of this opening session was deemed "overwhelmingly successful, if not miraculous" by several faculty members present. The enthusiastic participation of the whole group of seniors, followed by a dozen or more requests for opportunities to "experience that good feeling again," provided the final piece of evidence I needed. I knew then that further experiments were indicated.

A God-given opportunity came within a few months. Sister Kathleen Marie, Chairman of Drama at the College of Notre Dame of Maryland, having heard of the unusual Loyola incident, applied to the Maryland Committee for the Humanities and Public Policy for a special grant which would enable me to conduct a ten-week pilot project at the college. She hoped that this would, in her words, "prove the effectiveness of creative drama in reaffirming senior citizens' self-esteem and providing opportunities for creative growth." The project, called "Dynamic Living in Retirement," was funded in November 1976, and in February 1977 we started with a group of twenty-five men and women, black and white, aged sixty-one to eighty. Because we had accumulated another thirty names on a waiting list, the funding agency increased the grant to cover the cost of conducting a second session which began three weeks later.

Our cooperating observer-psychologist's evaluation offered the final affirmative testimony. In April 1977, he wrote ". . . . the participants spoke of the course as bringing a new energy, new hope, new confidence, and new life to them. . . . They eagerly accepted Mrs. Burger's call to open their eyes to what the present world offers, and drop their exclusive concern for self. She explained clearly how creative drama experiences induce self-forgetfulness and help one understand and relate to others . . . ."

Since April 1977 more chapters have been added to the story:

1. May 1977—I discussed our experiment at a nationwide gerontology symposium at the College of Notre Dame. It was received with great interest by the national delegates.

2. July 1977—I spoke about the benefits of the creative drama experience as part of a lecture series for seniors, sponsored by the Baltimore Community College.

3. August 1977—Members of the Greater Homewood Community Corporation (a city-sponsored agency offering senior programs), after hearing the July talk, arranged for me to conduct a ten-week project on "Dynamic Living" for their agency, September-December 1977; a second, similar project was scheduled for February-May 1978. Both were sponsored by the Catonsville Community College.

4. August 1977—At the American Theatre Association Convention in Chicago, I received a citation for this pioneer work with seniors. The announcement inspired letters and requests for information and materials from interested persons in six states.

5. September 1977-May 1978—Six individual seminars, lectures and/or demonstrations were given: to the Johns Hopkins Forum, Chapters of American Association of Retired Persons, the Advocates for the Aging, the Mid-Atlantic Chapter of ATA, and other senior programs. On May 24, 1978, I gave a workshop and demonstrations for the Maryland Gerontology Consortium at the College of Notre Dame.

6. February 1978-May 1978—The Maryland Committee was sympathetic to our second appeal for funds to extend the experiment to leadership training in creative drama and aging. Because of the hundreds of calls for assistance and materials, we knew that we must organize, analyze, and utilize the methods and materials we had found effective, working through potential leaders. Each applicant for the

training course was personally interviewed for selection. The final group represented, among others, program directors or leaders from senior centers, the County Commission on Aging, several nursing homes, and the Waxter Center of Baltimore. They met for ten consecutive Mondays from 10 a.m. to 2 p.m. The first hours were spent observing my work with a group of thirty seniors. During the final hour-and-a-half I discussed creative drama, its theory, methods, and materials with the trainees alone. These leaders have been most enthusiastic; some are already experimenting successfully with their new-found techniques.

7. Fall, 1978—I accepted an invitation to speak at a regional conference of the National Council on Aging and its Center for Arts and the Aging. The meetings, held in Hartford, Connecticut, examined all the arts, and considered how they could best be offered to benefit the aging. My talk, on the value of the creative drama experience, focused on the training of leaders for this field. It was warmly received. The enthusiastic response testified to the rising interest among senior center workers in finding printed material to assist them in their programming.

8. November 1978—The Baltimore County Department of Aging became interested in the possibility of planning training sessions for senior leaders at the College of Notre Dame. A meeting with the Senior Affairs Officer of the Department and the Continuing Education Division of the college resulted in an ambitious co-operative plan. I was to conduct a creative drama class for seniors, called, as before, "Dynamic Living in Retirement," during the spring semester, beginning February 1979. They would meet at the college on ten successive Monday mornings, February until April, from 10-11:30 a.m. The first twenty seniors to apply would be accepted. Twenty leaders, selected from Baltimore County's twenty-six senior centers' staff, would also

arrive at the college at 10 a.m. They would observe my work with the seniors. After that group was dismissed at 11:30, the leaders would meet with me in the classroom for discussion and careful study of creative drama techniques. The plan worked extremely well for both groups. The four leaders who requested college credit for the course paid tuition fees to the college; the others, interested only in the training, paid no fee, and were not required to take an examination or write a final thesis. Because of the success of the project, a plan for October 1979 includes the formation of three senior groups at Baltimore County locations under the leadership of three of the newly trained workers.

9. August 1979—At the American Theatre Association's annual convention in New York I was asked to serve on the newly formed Senior Adult Theatre Committee of the Children's Theatre Division of the ATA. During several hours of meetings, I exchanged ideas and experiences with colleagues from all over the U.S. We soon discovered how great was our sensitivity to the needs of seniors, and agreed that the creative drama experience can play an important part in filling those needs. Equally rewarding was the response to my talk on the second day of the convention, entitled "Adapting Creative Drama Methods for Use with the Aging."

To one who has devoted half a century to the study and practice of creative drama, discovering still another way in which this art can further human growth and development is exciting and gratifying. My fervent wish is to find a way to share the results of these challenging projects with other agencies both here and abroad.

Isabel B. Burger

August 1979

1
Gerontological Problems and Needs

To understand clearly how much seniors need renewal and refreshment of mind, body, and spirit today, one must examine some of the recent studies on aging and observe the general behavior of those with whom one comes into personal contact. A regrettable but generally accepted fact is the destructive effect of the present social attitude, building largely since the 1960's, expressed in the frequently heard statement: "It's dangerous to listen to people over thirty."

In the nuclear family, the separation of young people from their parents and grandparents has come to be expected. It is not surprising then, that in many of our seniors we see a withdrawal, an insecurity, a desire for isolation. And surely their sense of loneliness is to be blamed partially on the world's indifference. When a person feels useless, or robbed of a sense of purpose, the tendency is to build higher and higher protective walls, withdrawing from the outside world. Inactivity fosters concentration on the self, and one's woes and miseries are magnified. Soon, a feeling of hostility and increasing bitterness develops. This can change only if one feels needed and accepted by others—valued, welcomed, listened to with attention, respect, and kindness. Such was indeed the status of the ancient member of the tribe in societies of long ago. He was at once priest, sage, font of all wisdom—the respected and needed advisor and counselor. How different is his position today! Frequently the older person is not only *not* listened to, but many times he is not given the chance to speak. Few consider what he has to say either valid or worthwhile.

The general breakdown in the family structure, early retirement rules, and the extension of the lifespan by modern medical techniques and "miracle" drugs, have greatly contributed to the problem. There are thousands of lonely, bitter adults in the world, for whom life has become a miserable existence. Much of their time is spent in commiserating with themselves, expending their diminishing emotional energy on destructive thoughts of self-pity and self-hate. They begin to lose much of their curiosity, interest, and emotional response. The inactivity leads to inertia and boredom. Such a condition is aptly described by Gide when he says: "The spirit falls into boredom when it has no goal left . . . boredom's hideously inexpressive face we call anorexia."

Another result of this withdrawal and loneliness is a rigidity of mind and heart. One begins to feel uneasy about new ideas, new ways of living. Making choices and facing unfamiliar situations are frightening experiences to be avoided if possible. One prefers to fall back on old habits rather than to make adaptations and changes. One feels more secure when protected from the *catastrophic* interference of new ideas. Dr. Paul Tournier, Swiss psychiatrist, blames this isolation of the aging on the world in which we live: "The whole of society is sick with loneliness because it involves only superficial contacts. The loneliness that gnaws at the heart of so many old people is characteristic of the whole civilization and it condemns it."[1] According to Professor von Durckheim, when the Japanese were asked what they considered the supreme good in their country, they replied at once, "Our old people." The attitude of the western world in the twentieth century is

---

[1]Dr. Paul Tournier, *Learn to Grow Old,* (New York: Harper & Row, 1972).

exactly the opposite; and surely, the psychological state of the old depends, to a great extent, on the attitudes of those around them. Dr. Tournier comments further on this point, "Our sickness is the depersonalization of the modern world . . . we have given *things* priority over *persons* . . . . A civilization, which despises its old is inhuman."[2] There is indeed an alarming contrast between the wealth of technological progress and the poverty of human relationships.

A challenging question faces us all: how can we alleviate this distressing situation? Here creative drama enters the arena: creative drama with "adapted" techniques, as a contributive solution to some of the problems. Let us not deny the fact that many civic leaders are offering a variety of aids to seniors: socials, bingo games, free concerts, crafts, trips, and other like projects. All of these are acceptable as interesting, time-filling entertainment, but as spiritual and mental renewal and refreshment I feel they have little to offer. As an alternative, I am convinced that we have a real case for the creative drama experience as a motivator of the renaissance we all need. And here, let us understand what is meant by the term, "Creative Drama." (My apologies to those specialists who are already experts in the field!) My own definition, from my textbook, is, "The expression of thought and feeling, in one's own terms, through action, speech, or both." The key phrase is "in one's own terms." This means expressing what we think and feel in our own way.

But isn't this life, one might ask? Don't we do this all the time anyway? *Yes, we do,* as long as we can relate to people who love us and want to hear what we have to say. *Yes, we do,* as long as we feel that what we have to say is worthwhile. *Yes, we do,* unless we have become so suppressed in our aloneness and self-pity that circumstances have petrified our ability to think and feel imaginatively. It is not chronological

---

[2]Ibid.

age, but disuse, say the experts, that hampers the normal functioning of the brain. The brain, like the muscles, grows weak and ineffective from disuse. Imagination and creativity are eternal, the Creator's gift to every human being. They cannot die, but they can lie dormant and deprive us of those vital, exciting moments when the spirit lifts us on the wings of a new thought, or sound, or vision. And these moments are essential to every good life! Hundreds of scholars have stressed the significance of the imagination in a healthy, balanced, and fulfilling life. Einstein said, "Imagination is more important than knowledge; knowledge is limited, imagination embraces the whole world." How true an observation! At every moment of our lives we are having to adjust to what is happening around us; we are constantly called upon to make an imaginative response to an idea or set of conditions. Without experiences that strengthen and stimulate the imagination, one can end up by suffering a severe case of psychic malnutrition. The result is a kind of shallowness of spirit, ending eventually in a complete absence of humaneness and compassion.

As we grow older in today's society, original ideas seem suspect. Somehow we strive to suppress them and conform, until finally we lose altogether the power to do otherwise. It follows, then, that if we are to help our often lonely, tense, depressed, and uncommunicative seniors to lead happier, more interesting lives, we must find ways to activate the imagination, to dissipate the negative emotions, and to replace them with compassion, awareness, and responsiveness. Finally, we must help them to develop again their ability to express spontaneously their thoughts and feelings, thereby deepening their understanding and acceptance of themselves and their fellow human beings.

We must be guided, as we work, by some of the conclusions reached in the science of applied gerontology. First, the experts tell us, beware of the person who says, "I am looking forward to this retirement business! I can't wait to sit and do nothing!'' This kind of person needs help. He has probably done this same kind of ''sitting'' all his life, and has never tried any kind of self-expansion program. He has undoubtedly left all responsibilities to others. He is likely eventually to feel lonely, bored, and defeated; his physical condition may also deteriorate faster. It is interesting to note here that half the so-called senility cases are caused primarily by emotional disturbances, such as self-pity and self-hate. The key to positive, lasting health lies in a struggle rather than a retreat, involvement in rather than avoidance of the stress of living. It is ''doomsday'' for those who do not stay open to life and to a multiplicity of interests. There is direct physiological connection between persistent fear and tension, and the weakening of the total organism; there is chemical imbalance resulting from negative emotions. Words like *faith, hope, love,* and *grace* have physiological significance; the benevolent emotions are truly regenerative.

Let us look closely, then, at creative drama as a means to an end, a possible help to these lonely, closed, unhappy seniors. Since it involves the expression of thought and feeling, it seems a natural tool to adapt for this purpose. And once more, let us be clear about the difference between informal or *creative* drama, and formal theatre which involves play-production for an audience. The latter activity may offer pleasure to those seniors who, fortunately, have retained a positive self-image and have not succumbed to the destructive feelings of self-pity. Their confidence may still be abundant, and they may derive satisfaction in memorizing lines, attendance at rehearsals, and the supportive sound of audience applause. In my experience, the number of seniors ready for this sometimes tensing and demanding activity is very small. The great majority will tend to avoid signing up for any project listed as theatre or play-making. Thoughts like, ''I couldn't step on a stage'' . . . . ''I'd be scared to death'' . . . .

"I can't memorize anymore," are frequently expressed in a center where a formal play program is being discussed. For the ten percent of self-confident, extroversive spirits, this is a fulfilling activity. I suggest, however, that we should be more interested in the other ninety percent—those whose healthy self-concept seems to have diminished or vanished. They need desperately to revive their fallen hopes and to replace their empty days with active, happy ones.

It is for this reason that we called our pilot project at the College of Notre Dame "Dynamic Living in Retirement." Within a week of the first public announcement, we were deluged with applications. And is this surprising, really? Don't we all want to discover the secret of living dynamically? After careful evaluation, we feel justified in considering that all six groups meeting since February of 1977 have been very successful in terms of motivating positive growth and change.

USING CREATIVE DRAMA: CHILDREN VS. SENIOR ADULTS

In the succeeding chapters we will explore the step-by-step creative drama techniques adapted for these seniors. For all my readers, even those who practice creative drama regularly, I suggest a careful analysis of the essential difference in using this method with a group between the ages of sixty and eighty-five and with children or young adults. We have discovered, the hard way, how easy it is to err—to use a statement that will deaden enthusiasm, to move ahead too fast, to evoke fear tensions by using technical terminology. This book is based on very careful records, in which I have underlined the things that worked well and "red-penciled" the mistakes. For those leaders whose creative drama experience *has* been largely child-centered, as has mine, a few words here about my own indoctrination may prove helpful.

In embarking upon my initial voyage into these untraveled waters, my ship equipped only with my well-worn theories and practices, I decided it might be wise, at the outset, to examine the problems and goals of my former, familiar journeys into the land of children. Next, I analyzed the challenges, similarities, and differences involved with the new exploratory trip into the world of seniors. Would the same ship sail successfully in the deeper, more complex waters? That was the question to be answered.

Some of the results of this analysis and comparison follow here. First, the children—the juniors! What are they like? What are their needs in terms of growth and development which creative drama can fulfill? From the start, every child's center is self. He expects his wants satisfied at once; he seeks approval always; he is constantly calling attention to himself; his thoughts center on his own desires, adventures, and interests. This is all natural, normal, and to be expected. It is to the personal growth of these self-centered little ones that we, as teachers of creative drama, hope to contribute. Socially, the child also encounters problems in his early years. He is eager for companionship, but often is not able to accept or to be accepted by his peers because of the *self* forces that stand in his way. The selfishness of some children serves to isolate them, the timidity and fears of others may cut them off, too, from peer relationships.

One of our objectives, then, is to help the child overcome this natural self-centeredness and arrive at the state where he can accept himself as he is, be comfortable with that self and feel free to become aware of and interested in the people and things around him. He needs to be able to reach out, accept, understand, and identify with his peers. It is only then that he, in turn, will be accepted by them and the nourishing, enriching, creative interaction will begin.

Now, let us examine the seniors with the same care. Let us look at their problems individually and socially. First, we discover that many of them are also being hampered by self forces, the negative force of self-pity, largely due to feeling inadequate, insecure, useless, and lonely. Socially, the problem stems from the fact that there are often few friends and family members available to provide counsel and companionship. Those who are still nearby sometimes resent or ridicule the senior's ideas and outworn philosophies. His very presence is often considered a nuisance. In the face of these situations, he tends to withdraw for fear of being hurt; from this very seclusion which he seeks, comes loneliness, followed by self pity, which frequently takes the form of resentment and hostility.

Our objective, then, with the seniors is to renew self-esteem, develop the acceptance of self as a worthwhile individual, a child of God, who still has a great deal to contribute to his fellow man. The rebuilding of this faith, this belief in one's self, is more difficult with seniors, because sometimes their hurts go deep and they have built their protective walls very high. On a closer look, however, it appears that the same creative drama principles can apply here! As one is able, even for a few minutes at a time, to think and feel like another individual, one's own destructive self thoughts may disappear. A sense of renewal and release stirs and refreshes. This principle is as old as Aristotle's explanation of catharsis: when one feels strongly the emotions of another his own emotions are dissolved, or purged; they disappear momentarily.

When one has begun to accept himself, or "love" himself (and I speak of *Agape* love in this instance[3]), he feels relaxed and secure about reaching out to accept and love others. A lesson we all learned long ago is still true today; no one can love his neighbor until he has first learned to love himself! So, in both cases, the basic educational philosophy which has long motivated my work in creative drama is sound. It is

---

[3] *Agape* (from the Greek), the biblical term for the kind of love that "bears all things, believes all things, hopes all things, endures all things." (1 Cor. 13:7-8).

applicable to the solution of both generic problems, which originate in destructive self impulses. To change self-centeredness, self-pity and self-hate to self-acceptance and love seems to me to be the key to the success of the work with both age groups.

The methods to use, the best approach with seniors, the detailed procedures, require careful thought, flexible planning, and much experimentation. The remainder of this text concerns itself with these matters. Several general, practical points which proved invaluable to me follow here:

1. Enthusing a group of seniors and interesting them in participating is bound to be more difficult than such an effort applied to children; to the latter, playacting is second nature. An approach which I found successful will be discussed in detail in a later chapter.

2. Progress with the elderly must be slower, because, as mentioned earlier, their protective walls of isolation are often high and solid. In the beginning few may want or dare to risk a trip outside these walls.

3. For many seniors, security lies in sameness, repetition, holding on to old habits and traditions. Anything new presents doubts and fears. On the contrary, with children, anything new is an exciting adventure, a challenge to be accepted at once!

4. The fourth point is obvious but worthy of mention. Powers of imagination, concentration, and awareness have become lethargic or dormant through lack of stimulation. With children, they are ever alive and active. If we recognize this fact, we will work in the first classes with seniors to awaken and strengthen these powers, sharpening sensitivity, responsiveness, and creativity.

5. Another subtle difference appears as we work with seniors. For many of them, the need for spiritual and psychological

support and enrichment is urgent. Teenagers, it is true, are also often seeking ideals and to establish a firm philosophy. But seniors, approaching their last decades of life, are in desperate need of reinforcing their faith, their spiritual values, and their hope for eternal life. Discussing such matters freely, providing them with inspirational thoughts, proved most important to all of our groups. This practice inspired many of the members to bring along their own favorite proverbs to share with the group. We thoroughly enjoyed compiling what we called our "Guideposts for Dynamic Living." I found that a few minutes devoted to positive, inspirational talk, set an optimistic, joyous mood for every class.

6. Creating and sustaining a climate of friendliness, love, and caring is essential for both juniors and seniors, but for seniors, many of whom long for compassionate under-standing and love, this atmosphere is vitally important. A welcoming smile, a gentle embrace, a few tender words of greeting, can go a long way toward creating the climate of freedom and relaxation in which creativity can flourish.

To sum up—as we compare philosophies and objectives, we find that work with juniors and seniors has much in common:

A. In both groups, the basic objective is to build a healthy self-concept in order to motivate enriching, creative human relationships.

B. In both groups, the best way to be comfortable with and love one's self is to get rid of self-pity, self-hate, self-pride.

C. In both groups, one of the most successful methods to use in eliminating self-centeredness is to become other characters, to think and feel as they do.

With care in searching out appropriate materials, adapting

them to appeal to this special age group, we who believe in the effectiveness of the creative drama experience should anticipate the same success with seniors as has been ours with children.

2
Creative Drama Philosophy

Before meeting with any group of seniors each one of us must take an honest analytical look at himself as a potential leader. Am I personally qualified? How do I need to change? What do I need to learn? These are only a few of the important questions which must be answered truthfully. To facilitate this process, I am including here some of the beliefs, attitudes, skills and philosophies which in my experience have proved essential for the successful leader:

1. One must care deeply about people! One must take genuine satisfaction in helping to motivate growth and change, and in bringing joy to every life touched through understanding, compassion, and love (in the sense of *agape—see p. 20).*

2. The successful leader must be emotionally mature, relaxed, secure, comfortable with himself, enthusiastic, self-confident but humble, imaginative, aware, spontaneous, and positive in his philosophy.

3. A strong spiritual quality, a deep faith, firm integrity, and high ethical standards are important assets. If the light of God's love shines through one's work, it will comfort, warm, and inspire lonely hearts. One of the seniors in a recent group said one day: "You know, I just couldn't get along without God!" Her face shone with joy when I replied, "I couldn't either, my dear, I really couldn't!"

4. A skilled leader needs a firm grounding in the principles of philosophy, psychology, human development and the science of gerontology.

5. Essential, too, is some familiarity with all forms of drama. Without adequate knowledge in this field, one will have difficulty selecting, adapting, and presenting interesting and workable dramatic moments from life or literature to serve as exercise material. A person should feel comfortable about playing through situations he has suggested if the occasion arises.

6. Only the leader who understands the accepted order of procedure in the creative drama project, namely, the process from a single beginning with pantomime to a complex conclusion involving improvised dialogue, will be effective in keeping the group happily participating. Moving along too fast, expecting too much, or too little, can nullify early successes. An individual's new awakening, at this stage, is like a very delicate flower; it needs tender, wise, supportive nurturing.

7. The honest leader in this field must have high professional standards. He will apply himself seriously to his project because he is sensitive to its significance. He will evaluate himself, adapting and changing where necessary. One would hope that he would prepare himself to assume eventually the responsibility of teaching other qualified leaders to use these techniques. Whether he works in an agency, senior center, or home for the aging, as volunteer or professional staff member, he must never forget that he is in the responsible position of being able to enrich and even extend life. Nothing is more urgent—more important!

A general comment on the composition of a group of potential workers in this new field may be in order here. Members of the pilot training project, conducted at the College of Notre Dame of Maryland, where the material in this book was first used successfully, represented widely

diversified backgrounds. This may be typical of interested
participants in future training sessions. Two were program
directors from nursing homes; one was an activities super-
visor at a retirement center; another was a retired nun,
responsible for planning activities for retirees in her order;
three were volunteers from community centers for the aging;
another was activities director for the Waxter Center for
Seniors (a city-sponsored program in Baltimore); a ninth was
the coordinator of programs for the Baltimore County Commission on Aging; still another was activities director for the
local housing authority. Interestingly enough, there were also
two former actor/director individuals who had become interested in using their professional skills to help refresh and
cheer senior citizens. Several in the group held master's
degrees in education or social work and were taking courses in
gerontology. It was obvious that the experiential background
of most members of this group was in the area of human
growth and development. Their greatest educational need was
in the field of drama. On the contrary, the two actors, already
well-versed in this field, might have needed help in the
humanities and social arts, psychology, and gerontology. One
draws interesting conclusions from this experience; the
practice of creative drama for the senior adult is complex. It
represents a challenging opportunity and a serious responsibility to the instructor. Thoughtful preparation and study in
several related areas are suggested.

At the first meeting one may encounter a group of perhaps
twenty-five seniors between the ages of sixty and eighty-five.
Some will have come on their own, interested in the free sessions, the title of the project (in our case it was "Dynamic
Living in Retirement"), the convenience of the location to
which bus transportation from the town center has been provided, or for any number of other reasons. From the outset,
the climate and the appeal of the general surroundings—the
warmth, informality, and physical comforts—are all ex-

tremely important. It is the leader's responsibility to set the stage, create the friendly climate, greet each arrival with enthusiasm and joy, indicate coat racks and places for canes and wheelchairs. He must make everyone feel welcome and completely at home. With a prepared list of registrants in his hand, he may be able to recognize some individuals, to introduce those he knows to others, and to exert every effort to be hospitable. The above suggestions apply chiefly to a heterogeneous group gathering at a central location for ten or more hour-and-a-half sessions on a weekday morning. If the members of a residential facility, day-care center, or nursing home are meeting in their own recreation lounge, the hospitality factor need not be stressed, since they already feel at home. There may still be hesitation, however, some curiosity and even some negative feeling about the new program and its leader; warmth, enthusiasm, and caring are still vital ingredients of the success of that first day!

The leader's goal, at the outset, is to develop a sympathetic understanding and a closeness within the group. It is helpful to discuss openly some of the problems that most of those "past-sixty" face in today's society. Most people would agree that there has been an over-emphasis on youth over the past few decades. People want to stay young, dress young and look young, and only to the young and middle-aged are the most responsible positions open. Thanks to the new drugs we live longer; yet, unfortunately, in many ways we seem to be appreciated less. Few seniors are welcome in the homes of younger relatives, a situation which often gives them a sense of insecurity, uselessness, and diminishing estimation of their real worth. As the sensitive leader discusses these unhappy but realistic attitudes, he will often notice a comforting nodding of heads in agreement. Most seniors are happy in the realization that the group leader sees, acknowledges, and sympathizes with their anxieties and troubles.

This is the moment to introduce an optimistic challenge. A

remark like the following may help: "If we continue to with-draw, feeling unwanted sometimes, and a little like a fifth wheel on a cart, we will finally destroy ourselves with self-pity. Instead we must realize that we have much to offer to this world, much wisdom gathered over many years of experi-ence." Many wise researchers have expressed encouraging and interesting thoughts on aging. The effective leader will find a way of using some of these ideas at the very beginning. Such thoughts will serve as bricks in the building of a firm, new foundation of self-confidence and a healthy self-concept. This process is vital to growth and change. Here are a few that may prove useful:

1. "To grow old means to begin a new occupation; it is a process of involvement into a new and different phase of life." (Goethe)

2. "Old age can be a time for ripening rather than decay." (George Sand)

3. Some of the best work of their careers was achieved after seventy by: Clemanceau, Verdi, Voltaire, Adenauer, and others.

4. Recent experiments have proven that the brain needs only exercise and regular use to keep it functioning as well at seventy as it did at forty. It is only inactivity, as in the case of muscles, that causes atrophy and deterioration.

5. Colonel Saunders, the Kentucky Fried Chicken king, started his multimillion-dollar business at age sixty-five with his first social security check.

Some conversation based on this cheery information will begin to establish, for every participant, the conviction that the senior segment of society is a rich source of wisdom, sound ideas, and balanced judgment which any flourishing civilization should use as a resource in building for the future. As Dr. Reuel L. Howe wrote recently, "We seniors are the largest unexploited human resource available to society. They need us.''[1] This statement emphasizes the fact that every individual alive has unfulfilled potentials to create and imagine. Creativity, that precious gift from our Creator, never dies; it will rust away, however, from disuse. Another quality, possessed by all, is a natural sense of curiosity, a seeking after knowledge. The interest in exploring new ideas never ceases if it is nourished and constantly stimulated. If the creative urge is given free rein, one can achieve a measure of self-realization that is more satisfying than anything previously experienced.

These thoughts lead naturally to a consideration of the full development of the whole person, and the part that is played by continuing, warm, human relationships. With many seniors, especially those living alone, this part of their lives is diminished or non-existent. Its significance, nonetheless, cannot be emphasized too strongly. Two great comments on this subject have been made by wise philosophers. Harry Overstreet said: ''The way for a human being to save himself is to grow into the fullness of his powers and into the knowledge that the greatest of these is *love.* '' And from Dr. Paul Tournier, the Swiss psychiatrist, come these words,'' . . . only through living dialogue between man and man and between man and God can the authentic whole person be realized.'' Both of these statements point up the vital need for continuing human relationships, creative interaction, and spiritual growth.

During this preliminary discussion, the seniors will begin to develop a new sense of their own worth and the realization that they can grow and change and contribute. Hopefully they will already have begun to wonder how they can put some of these ideas into practice. The time has come, now, to give them some specific suggestions and directives. Here are a

---

[1] Reuel L. Howe, *Stay Younger While Growing Older,* (Waco, Texas: World Books, 1974).

few that have proven most useful:

1. Let us learn to accept and respect ourselves. Self-respect is a prerequisite to earning the respect of others. If we will truly love and accept what we are and what we are going to become, we must cast off the crippling chains of self-pity, self-hate, and all doubts, fears and suspicions. These negative emotions can only build the walls higher, those walls that isolate us and prohibit healthful human relationships.

2. One gathers courage and strength as one breaks away from the "poor me" attitude and begins to live creatively, with a new sense of wonder, vitality, belonging, and imaginative responsiveness.

3. It is important that we clearly understand the difference between self-love, which is essential, and self-centeredness which is destructive and must be abandoned. The two are exact opposites. Love of self means having a healthy sense of one's own worth as a person. From this base we can reach out generously to others, accepting and loving them as we have learned to love ourselves. We will feel free to offer understanding and compassion. It is at this very moment that we start on the road to becoming whole, mature human beings.

4. Let us search diligently for opportunities to motivate creative growth. A new life begins as we open our minds and hearts to those about us and take the risk of abandoning some of the old customs and traditions on which we have relied for so long. Rebirth of creativity comes from personal, not technical, influences.

5. Commitment is all-important! It is an indispensable asset for the older adult who is trying to live creatively. An indifferent, uncommitted life is a dull and chaotic one. Indiffer-

ence adds to one's own, and the world's ills. I think of an old adage, often repeated to me as a child, which goes something like this: "Evil can only happen when good men do nothing." So let us begin to care deeply, to open eyes and ears and hearts, and to be aware, sensitive and curious! A person can only be creative as he widens his circle of interaction with others.

6. Seek to reaffirm a sound positive faith and practice it. Re-examine values and standards. Sharpen integrity!

This last point needs emphasis and further discussion. Reaffirming faith and re-establishing values is often extremely difficult for the senior adult who has few old friends or family members with whom he can discuss such vital, fundamental questions. He feels separated from the young world, a stranger in a strange land, where values, morals, and faith seem almost non-existent. It is therefore important for the leader to give extra support in this area by offering every possible opportunity for a discussion of some of the fundamental truths. He must not be hesitant to express his own faith, regardless of the background or religious affiliations of his class members. I have personally found enthusiastic acceptance of my reaffirmation of such ancient directives as the words of Jesus of Nazareth expressed to his own disciples: "A new command I give unto you, that you love one another." At first glance, such a statement may sound like fantasy, especially in a world where the word "Love" has been so perverted by misuse. But twentieth-century psychiatrists have admitted that this statement shows the most profound insight into human nature that has yet been achieved. They contend that man is in sound psychological health to the degree that he relates affirmatively to his fellow-man. Again, a comment from Dr. Reuel L. Howe clearly bears out this point of view: "Our love for people is the measure of our love for God. This kind of compassion moves us, transforms us, fills us with enormous capacity for good will toward men."[2]

It is quite possible that some readers, upon reaching this point in the text, will be asking such questions as, Where does creative drama come in? Why all this philosophizing? Is this discussion of attitudes and faith, self-pity, and deepening human understanding an intrinsic part of a creative drama project with seniors? The answer to this last question is yes and deserves further elaboration here.

The project whose leader does *not* begin by assessing the mental, moral and spiritual attitude of the participants is doomed from the start. The findings of a sensitive analysis will likely reveal the fact that many individuals, unhappily, possess some or all of the following characteristics: they are withdrawn, bitter, cynical, insecure, doubting, lonely, incommunicative, and unresponsive. A life governed by these attitudes is a half-life, isolated, negative, and destructive. The leader's first responsibility, then, is to effect change, through building a close, friendly relationship with his group. He will admit to the problems involved with aging and try to explain the possible reasons for their existence. His next step must be the offering of refreshment, guidance, encouragement, and specific suggestions for renewal, growth, and change. Only then, when heads are held a little higher, smiles replace frowns, and eyes shine with hope and confidence, does one dare to ask for active participation and the spontaneous expression of thought and feeling.

All of these preliminary hours are wisely spent in developing a climate for creativity, where love and caring release tensions and disperse self-consciousness and fears. A few remarks gathered from questionnaires, submitted by seniors in our pilot project "Dynamic Living in Retirement," give convincing evidence of the value placed on this pleasant, comfortable atmosphere. These were replies, in part, to the

[2]Reuel L. Howe, *Man's Need and God's Action,* (Greenwich, Connecticut: Seabury Press, 1958).

question, What did you especially enjoy about our time together?

"Joy, peace, happiness." "Your unique quality of expressing love for others." "The bonhomie of the group." "I feel more free to express myself in love instead of violence." "Just as when you go to church—I get a lift for the week." "I liked the openness and acceptance of each other." "The ease we found in engaging in conversation with other members." "The warm, loving feeling of one human being sharing the gifts of God-given creativity with total strangers has proved an inspiration." "The congenial, pleasant people." "The open friendliness of the group is tremendous." "I anticipate each Monday. I feel more alive and aware than I have for some time." "The joy of cooperating, communicating and sharing so completely with others." "There was such a beautiful feeling of freedom and congeniality."

Replies like these from more than a hundred senior adults, collected over a period of about two years, barely mention creative drama, the techniques used to help bring about the inner growth which they all seemed to cherish. They were, however, obviously impressed deeply by the warm, loving, free atmosphere, the wealth of creative, human interaction, all of paramount importance in accomplishing the personal change and renewal which is the conscientious leader's basic objective.

The seniors, now well aware of their own needs, are eager to discover some specific remedies to cure their self-pity, isolationism, insecurity, and cynicism. This is the time to introduce creative drama as one of the experiences which may ease some of the discomforts. Unless it is done very skillfully and tactfully, however, it may be received with doubt and hostility. One must be able to relate convincingly the creative drama technique with achieving the long range goals brought to light during the previous sessions. This is not as difficult as it sounds, for casting off the chains of self-centeredness and self-pity has already become the core of the objective. And what better way to forget self than to "try on" another character, thinking his thoughts, responding to his feelings? It is usually necessary to admit from the start that some of the activities being shared will seem strange and perhaps even purposeless. Ask for faith and trust from the participants; express absolute conviction, backed up by concrete experiences, that wonderful things will happen! Senses will quicken, compassion, curiosity, and enthusiasm will be motivated; affirmative, rather than negative, emotions will govern behavior patterns. Assure everyone that each will participate only when he wishes, but make a strong plea for active response, arguing that the more one is involved the greater will be his progress. Explain the importance of working together freely and honestly sharing thoughts and feelings. Because they care, they can help one another discover ways of living happier more contributive and dynamic lives. This and this alone is the leader's objective! The purpose is *not* to learn a skill or craft, like weaving, gardening, acting or singing; nor is it to entertain. Rather, the objective is to help everyone to become the most that he is capable of becoming and to remain a person of worth to himself and to society as long as he lives.

An introduction which has proven successful is a discussion of some universal truths about the beginning of theatre. These ideas need not be called theatre history but rather the story of man's need for communication. It has long been known that for all people, since the beginning of time, there has been a desperate need for man to communicate with his fellow man. The expression of thoughts and feelings have been basic to health and happiness. Dance, music, song, drama have offered avenues of expression of man's deepest emotions and his search for the essence of the meaning of life. In his ritual dance, or dramatic movement, he has thanked the gods for victory, begged for rain, or rejoiced in the good harvest. One can conclude from these facts that everyone, even in our civilized society, needs to find some basic form of expression to release his innermost thoughts and feelings. Creative drama has been selected as our preferred medium because it has proven to be so helpful in furthering relaxation and in building the self-confidence, awareness, responsiveness, and sensitive human understanding which can bring a person closer to a fuller realization of his own potentials.

In order to plan successfully for the first simple exercises the leader will be well aware of the frightening loss of sensitivity in most aging individuals. The senses, quietly and without warning, fall into a sort of sleep, depriving one of all kinds of experiences and sensations which make life interesting and exciting. The power to concentrate also diminishes appreciably from disuse, and imagination often becomes dulled and inactive. The constant exposure to radio and television has accelerated decay in these areas. Programs jump from content to commercial and back again so often and so fast that one's concentration powers are taxed to the limit. When one relies so completely on canned entertainment, one no longer finds it necessary to call upon creative and imaginative skills. Since these skills continue to remain unchallenged and unused, they naturally deteriorate. They must be exercised back to normal health. These problems can be appropriately and tactfully brought to the attention of senior participants, so they will understand the importance of some of the simple pantomime exercises used at the beginning.

At a very early session, it is wise to agree on a few general rules, which will help the program run smoothly.

1. Let us make a mutual promise that when we come through this door, we will leave all "self" thoughts at home. These are the thoughts that separate and isolate us.

2. Try to banish all doubts about what we are doing and why. Just participate, enjoy, and believe! Something wonderful will happen!

3. Come on time and every time! Growth and change occur surely but slowly, as we grow older. It is a continuing process which needs regular weekly experiences to sustain and implement it. A serious relapse can be caused by missing one or two sessions. Here it may be wise to stress this need for perfect attendance at the very first session. This will provide an opportunity for those who may have come only out of curiosity to withdraw their names from the list.

4. Believe in positive results; believe that it will be exciting! This awakening of a new vital feeling about people and about yourselves is like suddenly discovering a new self, traveling down a new and pleasant path, into a new bright world!

We can now put our principles and prescriptions into practice as we are now ready to embark upon the first series of exercises and activities with the seniors.

3
Elementary Pantomime Activity

The time has come now to begin some simple activities in which all can participate. These must be introduced very carefully, accompanied by supportive help and hints which can be used profitably during all future sessions. The first of these, and most important, is an explanation of the two "Keys" to successful pretending. Application of these two basic rules exercises the powers to imagine and concentrate; this will guarantee sincere, believable results.

THE TWO KEYS

KEY 1: Make a clear picture in your mind. See the place where the action occurs (the meadow, the airport, the cellar, etc.) and see, in your imagination, all the objects you will find there or handle as the situation progresses. For example: if two old friends decide to meet, after thirty years, in a hotel lobby, they must see the heavy carpet, the low couches in the lounge, the bustling bellhops, the revolving doors, and other appropriate details.

KEY 2: Think the thoughts of the character you are playing. This means completely wiping out your own thought pattern. For example: in the scene just described, the first friend to arrive at the hotel lobby must replace her own thoughts with ideas such as these: "I wonder if we'll know each other, after all this time? I'm sure this is the place she said in her letter." (Here she would glance at the letter in her hand.) "There's such a crowd, I hope we don't miss one another. The clock says three; that's the time she suggested. Maybe I'll just sit on the couch over there where I can watch the door.'' These thoughts, appropriate to the character in such a situation, motivate body movement and tell us much about the first person to appear in the story, who she is and why she is here.

As potential leaders, let us consider the therapeutic value of this experience so far. Especially would I urge such thoughts upon the doubters who insist that one should provide only entertainment for seniors, not therapy. I feel called upon to remind those readers to remember that those who sincerely work to enrich the life patterns of the senior adult should constantly think of the therapeutic effects of their activities. In this simple exercise which has been described above, if the participant can truly eliminate all self thoughts, even for a few minutes, a genuine catharsis occurs; in a sense, the healing process begins. For the space of those few moments, he is inside the heart and soul of another, walking in someone else's shoes. He can no longer think of his own aching leg, his crotchety neighbor, or the bills he owes. He has freed himself, for this moment, of all destructive, negative thoughts.

As the leader explains the two *KEYS*, he may give examples himself. He may become the friend, waiting in the hotel lobby. When he is finished, he might ask the group to tell him what thoughts they could read in his face as he waited. In this way he can prove that specific thoughts will change facial expression and motivate appropriate body action. It may be necessary to give several examples like this one in order to drive the point home. Here are two which have worked well:

A. Let us imagine that I am baby-sitting, in an old farm-house, where my niece lives. I am there to stay with her little one so that she and her husband may attend a lovely concert in a neighboring town. Suddenly, as I sit quietly knitting, I hear a sound. It seems to come from upstairs.

    I think: "What is that? Sounds like footsteps. I'd better go investigate." Let the group observe how these thoughts affect your face and body movement.

B. Come home from work or from an errand, a little earlier than you expected. As you walk into the living room, you hear a conversation in the next room. The thoughts come: "Who's that talking? It's sister's voice . . . but . . . that other one? It's familiar . . . but *yes*! It's John. He's come back!" Your darling nephew has returned from Europe early and dashed over to see his favorite aunts. As you think: "What a lovely surprise!" You naturally hurry into the next room to greet John.

SOME SIMPLE GROUP EXERCISES

By this time, the participants will be eager to try to apply the two *KEYS* themselves. Some very simple group exercises should be selected which involve pantomiming a familiar activity. It is advisable to choose some imaginary situations which are both appropriate to the group's former experience, and also can be done together and in a sitting position. The effort to move the whole body, while pretending to be someone else, may in the beginning be too demanding. The following example may serve this purpose:

Let's pretend that today is everyone's birthday. Isn't it lucky that we all have the same birthdate? Well, to help celebrate, I have brought along some little boxes of fudge—one for each of you. I made it last night and packed these little boxes this morning. (Show, in pantomime the shape of the box, width and height.) They are all lined with wax paper. There are two layers of fudge and the remainder of the paper is folded over on top to keep the lid from sticking. (Demonstrate again!) There's a card on the top of the box with your name on it and "Happy Birthday," but there are no outside wrappings, ribbons or bows. (By making each detail very clear you facilitate the forming of an accurate "mind picture") Now . . . don't look yet! Wait until I give you the signal. I have put your boxes on the floor, just beside your chair. In a moment, when I say "Look!" reach down, find your box, put it in your lap, lift the lid off and put that in your lap. Then unfold the wax paper and pick up one big luscious piece of candy. You just can't resist it! Eat it all at once. Then fold back the paper, put the lid on and put the box back on the floor.

Emphasize the importance of seeing the box clearly before beginning the exercise. One might say, "See its shape and color and feel the texture and the weight as you pick it up. Look at the lovely card! See that thin wax paper as you take the lid off . . . and feel that smooth chocolate in your fingers . . . mmm! When you fit the lid back on, do it carefully!" Much of this detail should be stressed to reawaken the sense of sight, touch, smell, and taste. Be sure to remind the group that although they are all working together, each is to imagine himself alone. Each must concentrate on his own picture, think his own thoughts, paying no attention to his neighbors. Since everyone's thought patterns are different, the end of the exercise may come sooner for some than for others. This is to be expected! There is no right or wrong way to do it, nor any correct timing. For each participant, his own way, determined by his own thoughts, done in his own time, is correct. A warning here may help to develop concentration. If one looks toward his neighbor, watching his work, he will automatically introduce a different, disturbing thought, such as, Oh dear, he's nearly finished, I'd better hurry! Such an interruption will blot out his own picture and sometimes it is gone beyond the point of recovery! Another warning is also in order. If one is reaching for an imaginary box which he has discovered at his feet, any noise, whisper, cough, or laugh will completely dissolve the picture and abruptly destroy the thought pattern. The action, from that point on, will become automatic and unbelievable.

Above: Participants in a creative drama workshop "lifting" imaginary objects to their laps during a pantomime exercise. At right: One of the group members returning the "object" to the floor. Workshop conducted by Jennifer Vermont at Leonard Covello Senior Center in New York City. Photographs by Terry Buchalter. Courtesy of Brookdale Drama Project, directed by Milton Polsky.

It is important, therefore, to stress the need for silent concentration from the whole group. This may control the behavior of those with a tendency to giggle or whisper; there are always a number of persons whose disturbing chatter or laughter serve as a cover-up for their insecurity and embarrassment. It is wiser to ask, quite seriously, at the beginning for complete quiet, giving your reason—the need to preserve everyone's mind picture. Sometimes feelings are hurt, and the mood is broken if one must interrupt an exercise with a directive to "Stop laughing, please." If the leader makes his point clearly and seriously beforehand, he can often persuade the group to accept his advice and suggestions. At heart, they are all eager to be successful in their own first efforts to be convincing. Even these simple pantomimes are to be considered seriously; the goal is to make them believable. This is no game of charades! It is not "acting as if" but truly becoming! Herein lies its value.

At the conclusion of the "box of fudge" exercise, which should be done with the whole group, the leader should make some encouraging comments, perhaps something like, "Well, that was great! I could really see and taste some of these squares of fudge! And I could see the shape and weight of most of the boxes." To one member he might make a special comment, "I believe I saw your paper stick to the fudge, didn't I?" And perhaps to another who showed little concentration, "I have a feeling I lost the lid of your box, my dear. I thought you put it in your lap, but you picked it up from the floor." This evaluation or critique practice will accustom the group to the procedure which plays a significant part in this kind of project. A little later, four or five will attempt an exercise while the rest observe. This provides a fine opportunity for a group evaluation or critique of the performance. Knowing that one is expected to comment on a completed exercise, each individual will learn to sharpen his own concentration and observation powers so that he will have something to contribute to the general discussion. The ability to give and take constructive criticism is often a lost art, especially to overly sensitive senior adults; it is nonetheless important in building strong human relationships, one of the basic goals of the project.

An interesting way to involve everyone in the critique process is through the use of color cards. Cut from construction paper, in four colors, enough small 2″ x 3″ cards for everyone. Divide a group of twenty into four sections of five each. One section would be composed of those who drew green cards from the box, another the yellow card holders, a third those who held red cards and the fourth those with blue cards. The "greens" would be asked to comment on the work of the "yellows" and vice versa; the "blues" and "reds" would then work together. Although all participants are really watching every exercise, this arrangement narrows down the concentration responsibility to careful observation of only five people. Sometimes it is interesting to number each set of cards from 1 to 5. According to this plan, one would evaluate only the work of his corresponding number and color. For example, Green 2 would comment on Yellow 2. All of these procedures have specific and relevant objectives. First, through the random drawing of cards, it is easy to develop new relationships within the group and avoid the common practice of friends working only with friends. Second, powers of observation are sharpened when one is definitely responsible for commenting on another's work. Third, as the critique practice continues, every participant will gradually increase his power to organize his thoughts and express them more fluently.

It is important that everyone in the group be given a chance to do an exercise at every session. Unless some seem hesitant and prefer to be only observers for a while, the leader should attempt to have everyone experience the same or a similar pantomime situation. In a group of twenty to twenty-five (a larger group is not recommended), two or three exercises might be attempted during an hour-and-a-half session. The following situations have worked well during early meetings of the class when people feel free enough to move about. If space permits, groups of four or five can try each exercise. The leader will initiate a general critique after each group effort.

1. Let us imagine ourselves as refugees from an eastern country who have been brought to the U.S.A. by a sponsoring group of Quakers. Today a bus has been rented to take us to a beautiful apple orchard in the country, where we have been given bags and told to pick whatever we like. Never having seen apples growing before, this is a truly exciting experience. (The leader indicates where the bus has stopped and the direction into the orchard.) Come into the orchard, with your bags, and pick about a half dozen apples and then go back to the bus. (This kind of direction makes the beginning and ending of the scene a little more specific and gives the participants a feeling of security.)

2. We're spending a week or so at a friend's mountain cabin which, although beautiful and situated high above a clear lake, has no modern conveniences. All water must be brought in by bucket from a well near the house. Each bucket must be dipped by hand and carried to the porch. So let us each take an empty bucket from the porch (indicate the area) and carry it to the well. To make it easier each one will imagine his own well. (Indicate the position of the five wells and the height of the brick wall built around each.) When you feel your bucket filling, and becoming heavier and heavier, be sure to hold it tightly. Then lift it carefully and carry it back to place it on the porch.

3. In the same mountain camp, there is the problem of hanging out dish cloths and perhaps wet bathing suits to dry on a line stretched between two trees. (Indicate the area of the

line and be sure the space is adequate; five people should not feel cramped as they work together.) This scene starts when you come out of the cabin, carrying a small basket containing the two dish towels you have already washed and are about to hang on the line. There are clothes pins in your pocket or in the basket. When you have the towels safely on the line, pick up the little basket and go into the cabin again. (Indicate the entrance to the cabin.)

4. Let's imagine that you have some lovely pots of marigolds and zinnia seedlings on your kitchen window sill. You have been away and it is important that they have some water. Pick up the little watering pot from the drainboard. (Indicate the sink and drain along one side of the room. There should be room enough so that each of the five participants may have his own sink and window sill.) Fill the pot and water the thirsty little plants; empty out the remaining water and put the watering pot back on the drainboard. And don't forget to turn off the water!

The above material is provided merely as suggestions for simple activity pantomime. Any leader who knows his group members and their backgrounds and interests will be able to create dozens of such exercises which will be appropriate and challenging. Although it is impossible to make any fast rules about how long to use such simple material, it is important not to move to more difficult assignments until the whole group seems free, comfortable, and able to forget self and to use the two *KEYS* with ease. Perhaps two or three sessions will be devoted to this elementary beginning. Some groups, however, may be able to attempt complex mood exercises almost immediately. The leader must assume the responsibility for making this decision.

4
Movement and Mood

By the third or fourth meeting with the seniors, it will very likely be possible to use some more complex exercises which require additional movement and to start to play through some situations which call for the expression of a specific mood or emotion. The wise leader will be aware that only material that is appealing, understandable, and within the experience range of the group members should be used. They cannot be expected to recreate believably a situation which is vague or unfamiliar. Time must be allowed for a complete evaluation of each attempt, including spontaneous comments and suggestions from members of the group. From time to time the leader should refresh memories concerning the importance of using the two *KEYS*: (1) making a mind picture, and (2) thinking the thoughts of the characters being played. Questions like these will help, What would the park look like? Where would she put the basket? What might they think as they heard the knocking? This method helps them to put the *KEYS* into practice, and motivates believable thought patterns and actions.

An interesting exercise, involving two groups at a time, let us say the "yellows" and the "greens," concerns making purchases at a store—a delightful store where there is no charge for anything! The yellows will be the purchasers and the greens will be the recipients. The leader indicates the position of a long counter on a free side of the room: "There, you see that long counter over there? It has on it all kinds of lovely things to wear or to enjoy. I'd like five greens to line up here opposite the counter *(indicate this space)*. Now their five matching yellows, their number partners, will sit here *(indicate)* just behind your matching green number. The greens will proceed to the store counter, decide what you would like to have, select it, and bring it back, unwrapped, to your yellow partner. Now he will want to guess what you have brought him so you must handle your article in a way that your partner will be better able to know exactly what you have brought him.'' At this point the leader may want to facilitate things by a demonstration. He might go to the counter, select a book, a necklace, or a ring. As he turns and walks back toward the group he would open the book or put on the necklace or the ring. The participants will immediately guess and will be delighted that they can see the articles so clearly. The same exercise can be played with the ''blues'' and the ''reds'' and then the sections reversed; those who purchased will receive and guess. There is very little feeling expressed in this kind of pantomime, but it does demand much more imagination since each person must decide what he will select; in addition, he must handle it so carefully that his partner can also see it.

Before attempting any exercises in which stronger emotions motivate the movement pattern, the importance of expressing feelings should be discussed. As has been noted earlier, a person has far less opportunity for personal communication, as age deprives him of close relationships. He may also have lived through circumstances which have compelled him to suppress his feelings. Senses often become dulled; responses to any stimulus are therefore slower and smaller. We have found it extremely helpful to talk openly about how interdependent we are, how much we need one another and how precious are the warm, sincere human relationships we develop as we go along life's way. Troubles and pain are lessened when we can share them; burdens are lightened when someone else understands. Joys and satisfactions are magnified ten times over when someone who cares shares them with us. These universal and generally accepted statements lead inevitably to the conclusion that one cannot expect sympathy or help in time of trouble, unless one has communicated his problem, expressed his anxieties. And, by the same token, no one can rejoice with another unless he knows the other's cause for joy. Finally, a person must be able to communicate his feelings honestly and sincerely if he is to develop and profit from deep, rewarding human relationships. For many, this means working to keep the emotional mechanism active and responsive, otherwise faculties will become so dulled from disuse that they will become numb, wooden creatures, incapable of sensitivity or compassion.

The exercise material introduced at this stage will include various moods and changes of mood. Especially for those whose feelings have been sharply reined in and suppressed, this group setting is a comfortable place to begin to communicate again. Here, in this world of the imagination, we may be angry, afraid, resentful, jealous, joyful, or suspicious without threat of retaliation or unhappy consequences. Here, indeed, we can find the release and refreshment which long ago Aristotle described as "catharsis." When one feels and expresses a strong emotion as another character, he is simultaneously cleansed of many of his own blocked emotional tensions. A skillful British drama teacher, who has done some interesting work in creative drama with young people, describes this process vividly and convincingly: ". . . . this is a healthy letting off of steam! The throwing of a stone through an unpleasant neighbor's window is much better done in drama class than with a real stone in actuality . . . there is now ample evidence that enacting the deed in pretense, reduces the impulse to do it in reality."[1]

---

[1] R. N. Pemberton-Billing and J. D. Clegg, *Teaching Drama,* (London: University of London Press, Ltd., 1966).

Many interesting thoughts came from members of our groups during this discussion of moods and feelings. One very dear, vital eighty-six-year-old woman in one of my recent classes asked if she could add a comment about self-expression which she felt I had omitted. I agreed, of course. This was her remark: "I think it's very important to let what we feel come out, but I'd like to suggest that, even though we all have feelings, strong ones sometimes, we don't all have the same way of releasing them. You see, I have to express what I feel in poetry. Sometimes when I can't sleep, I feel so strongly about something that I just have to get up and write it down. As soon as I have expressed those feelings on paper, I can go right to sleep." This perceptive addition to the discussion soon brought thoughts from other members about painters, musicians, dancers, and sculptors whose feelings came forth in their chosen art form. After about a half hour's lively conversation, we all agreed that to be healthy and happy one *must* find a way to feel deeply and express fervently. Today's cultural patterns encourage superficial emotional response. We are constantly exposed to relationships and entertainments that only titillate the feelings. This subconsciously motivates us to build protective inhibitions; we tend to avoid anything which stirs more than a superficial reaction. And this is dangerous.

The groundwork laid, a start can be made with movement motivated by several moods. It is advisable to use eight or ten people at a time or even the whole group, if space permits. An interesting beginning can involve just walking in several different moods. The following exercise has been used very successfully.

Eight of you will start at this end of the room. Let's imagine, as you walk across to the other end (indicate positions here), that you are going home from your small-town post office. Since today is your birthday, you had hoped to find in your mail box a note or a card from your dear grandson who always remembers. This year he is in Europe studying, but you still go to the post office with great hope. Unfortunately, the box was empty, except for a few advertisements. How do you feel as you go down the street toward home? What are some of your thoughts? (Accept spontaneous suggestions from the whole class. When you feel that they clearly understand, proceed to the next part.)

Now, when you get to this other end of the room, which is home (indicate again), turn around, stop your thought pattern, for you will become someone else. This time as you move forward, you are entering the living room of a beautiful little beach cottage which your son has acquired and furnished for you and your friend. It is near his summer home and is exactly what you have wanted for many years. It is decorated in your favorite colors. And, remember, you are seeing it for the first time. Now, when you finish the thoughts in this second part, stand quite still, until I say "curtain" which is the cue to end the scene. Any movement, even a quiet return to your seat, may disturb someone else who has not quite finished.

In these two "walking" exercises, the basic mood in the first section is obviously disappointment; in the second, it is surprise and joy. Other simple situations of this nature can be attempted by large groups; they provide an easy and effective way of expressing feeling by simple movement. Always lead a critique with those who have been observers. To facilitate this kind of exercise and help motivate sincere thought patterns it may be wise to ask questions such as, What would you be thinking when . . ., or What are your thoughts as you take your very first look into that door? Soon it will be clear to everyone that it is the thoughts, in each situation, which govern the rhythm and pattern of body action. When one thinks, Oh dear, I guess he's too busy to remember his old grandma, the body will droop, the steps will be slow and heavy. In the second case, thoughts like, How beautiful! And look at that cheerful yellow . . . I can watch the sea from my window, move the body in swift, joyful rhythms; the head is high, eyes dancing, light footsteps seem scarcely to touch the ground.

A simple activity like gathering apples from low branches or windfalls from the ground can provide a fine opportunity for examining the effect of mood on body action. The assignment can be given this way:

Let us come out onto the porch here, pick up a basket, and go out into the yard where there is a small apple orchard filled with delicious ripe fruit (indicate the location of the porch, the orchard and the trees). We will divide into three groups, all three of which will do the same action, that is picking apples from the trees or from the ground and putting them into the basket. Each of the three groups will be different kinds of people picking apples under different circumstances.

Now, listen carefully! Group A, you have been visiting a friend who has a big farm and to express gratitude for your visit, you have promised to help with the daily chores. So far the promise hasn't been difficult to keep; today, however, is a different matter altogether! You're in the midst of watching an exciting mystery on TV and your hostess suddenly decides she must make an extra apple pie for dinner for unexpected guests. She asks you to pick a half a dozen more apples. How would you feel? What would you think as you started out to pick the apples? (Get replies from the group.)

Group B, your granddaughter has just called to say that she is bringing an important friend home for dinner and begs for one of Grandma's famous apple pies. You're having a touch of your wretched arthritis and have been lying down. Now you've no choice but to get yourself out to the orchard somehow. You simply can't disappoint that granddaughter whom you adore. But, with an aching back and an hour's notice, things are difficult! Thoughts like this might pass through your mind, Why on earth didn't she tell me before? I don't see how I'll have time to get a decent pie baked! My poor back! If only this weren't one of my bad days! Thinking these and similar thoughts will make your body and face move in such a manner that they will tell us a believable story.

Group C, you are poor vagabonds, wanderers, out of work, living from hand-to-mouth, sleeping under the stars or in some old deserted barn. Food has been scarce lately! Suddenly you spot a beautiful orchard, full of weeds, because it surrounds what seems to be an old deserted house. Decide, at once, that you must slip in through a break in the fence, and snatch a couple of those beautiful red apples. Thoughts will be very different this time, perhaps, Look at those gorgeous apples . . and I'm starving! That old house seems to be deserted. . . . Guess I'll just slip in through the fence. . . . I don't see anyone—no sign of life anywhere. . . . Better be quick about it. As you cautiously enter the orchard, fill your pockets with apples, and when you think you have enough, hurry out before anyone sees you.

COLOR AND RHYTHM IN MOOD EXPRESSION

An interesting approach to expression of mood is a discussion of the effects of color and rhythm on feelings. Often simple questions like, What color is anger? What color is joy? (or hope, or fear), will bring spontaneous, similar replies from the whole group. Most people think of happy moods belonging to the cheerful, yellow-red end of the spectrum, while the negative feelings fall largely into the blue, purple, and black tones. Another way of analyzing feelings is to consider their differing rhythm patterns. The happy traveler's step will be light, fast, and even; the steps of the sad or disappointed individual would be heavy, slow, and regular. In a mobile group of seniors, I have had good results with using a simple rhythm pattern of four measures of 4/4 time. After playing out the four measures on a drum, or make-shift drum (a coffee can with a plastic top serves very well), I will ask for ideas about what could be happening to these rhythms. The following four measures motivated some very interesting responses:

First measure	One whole note	1 - - -
Second measure	Two half notes	1 - 1 -
Third measure	One whole note	1 - - -
Fourth measure	Four quarter notes	1 1 1 1

One member of the group gave this story, suggested to her by the above rhythm pattern: A lady is in a strange town walking down the street trying to find her friend's house. She can't see the numbers over the doors very well because it is nearly dark, so she starts one step, and then stops for three beats while she examines the number (first measure). Then she walks two slow steps, still looking (second measure). Since neither of the houses is right, but the numbers are close to the one she wants, she looks closely at the next house (third measure). It *is* the right house so she hurries up the steps (fourth measure).

This dramatic situation fits very well with the rhythm pattern. There are many others that may be suggested, each involving several changes of thought and feeling, represented by the changing rhythm patterns. To discover a variety of situations which might be adapted to the same four measures is often an interesting and challenging experience. If a leader is not familiar with the use of rhythm, and does not feel comfortable about initiating this kind of exercise, it is wiser just to touch upon the changing rhythm and colors of moods, rather than attempt to act out and develop story material based on specific rhythms.

CONTINUING WORK WITH MOOD PANTOMIME

Although it is impossible to provide all the material which any leader will need for his seniors, since the composition of each group is so different, it may be helpful to make a few suggestions here for continuing the work with mood and change-of-mood pantomime. These exercises have been successfully used in our "pilot project" and may be adapted to the needs of other groups. It is very important, during this early stage to make one fact very clear to the participants— *There is no right or wrong way to express anger, fear, joy, hope, or any strong emotion.* Each of us will have his own personal rhythm, and for each, this is the believable, convincing reaction.

1. Use the two groups of five each. (The recommended method of using greens and yellows with numbers will serve here.) Each member of each group will select a small white slip from an envelope which will be passed around. On each slip a "mood word" is written, for example, *Anger, Surprise, Anxiety, Joy, Boredom,* etc. Each will be asked to think of a specific situation, which could be played in pantomime, in which the mood on his card would dominate. For example, the word is "Anger." Someone sees the bus coming, rushes to the corner but the bus, the last for an hour, goes by without stopping. He is furious! The five greens may be asked to begin. If there is space they will all work at once. Before starting they will match their numbers with their counterparts in the yellow group. Yellow 1 watches Green 1, Yellow 2 watches Green 2, and so on. At the end of the exercise, each yellow tries to guess his green counterpart's mood assignment. The leader must be ready to help out in these critique periods, so that the less communicative will not feel inadequate in any way. When this first trial is over, the observing yellows have their chance and their green partners will guess the moods expressed. The same exercise will then be done with the blues and reds and any other sections of the group until everyone in the room has had an opportunity to play the scene. During this kind of project the leader must be very definite on one point: one never tries merely to show anger, or act angry, by artificially shaking fists or resorting to other

cliché movements. There must always be specific imaginary reasons for one's feelings; these each individual must create for himself. When he has done this and applied the two KEYS and really does think the thoughts of the person in his imagined situation, the thought patterns will be real and will motivate honest, believable body action.

2. Using the same or a similar group plan, the following exercise can be interesting. Each member of the first group imagines himself coming into his house in the afternoon happy over something he has just bought or perhaps heard. He finds a written message on a table near the door. As he reads it, his mood changes. Let the player's counterpart guess what the note says and why the mood has changed in each case. On the next try, those who have guessed become the active players, and the members of the first group guess the reasons for the mood change.

3. A challenging mood pantomime can be set in an airport or railroad station of a small town. The leader presents it this way: You are in the (airport or station) to meet someone whose arrival is imminent. You must decide who is being met, your relationship with the individual and how you feel about this meeting. Are you happy to see this person, or afraid perhaps? Are you sad to have to give him bad news about a relative, or curious to see how much he has changed after all these years? Make your decision before you start to play. As we watch you, waiting in the airport, we should be able to see, by your thoughts, how you feel about this meeting. Then, suddenly, you hear a message over the P.A. system that "Flight #123 will not come in today. There has been an un-avoidable delay because of weather." (The leader will make this announcement at an appropriate time.) How will you feel when you hear the announcement? Are you disappointed, glad, terribly angry? Your partner will watch closely to see if he can guess who your expected visitor is and how you feel

Two examples of mood expression in a particular dramatic situation. At left: Workshop participant recalls in pantomime how she felt upon receiving a particular birthday present as a teenager. The exercise, called the "Magic Birthday Box," is conducted in Abbe Raven's workshop at Katherine Engel Center for Older People in New York. Below: The same participant reveals a more solemn and dignified mood as she complies with a request to conduct a symphony orchestra in concert. Photographs by Terry Buchalter. Courtesy of Brookdale Drama Project, directed by Milton Polsky.

and what you will do about his failing to appear. (This exercise can also be done with five or six at a time, if there is sufficient space. The critique period after each attempt offers an excellent opportunity for each player to tell his own story, the imaginary traveler he has conceived, and the relationships which existed between them.)

4. The action for this pantomime is very simple: Pull a full-length curtain over a large window. The purpose of such an exercise is to stimulate each individual's imagination and challenge this creativity. One might introduce it this way: Now I shall ask each of you to imagine yourself in a room which has a long window and full-length drapes, on rings, which slide easily on a large rod. In other words, the curtains can be opened or closed by hand. The action is merely the closing of the curtains. We want to guess why you are closing them. You have a very definite reason, in your situation, to want them closed. Be very specific in your planning and your thoughts or we shall never be able to guess your reason. You will find it helpful to answer these questions for yourself before you start: Who am I? Where am I? Why am I here? Why do I want the curtains closed? You may start sitting down, listening to music, perhaps, or sewing, or knitting, or whatever you like. Then get the thought about closing the curtains. We should be able to guess the answers to your questions. (Try this with small groups and assign one person to watch each one. Let each player explain his complete situation during the critique period. There are several reasons for this practice: 1) When a player can explain his dramatic situation in words, the leader can be sure that he has developed a specific reason for his reaction; 2) Giving each player a chance to enlarge on his special dramatization is satisfying and helps build his affirmative self image.)

This chapter has introduced mood movement and body response—some of it quite complex in nature. The importance of expressing feeling has been discussed and the need to deepen human relationships by becoming more sensitive and responsive has been stressed. The connection between moods, rhythm, and patterns of body movement has been clarified and varied exercises have required the participant's imagination to provide the background situation motivating mood response. By this time the leader will usually notice, in all members of the group, a new freedom, relaxation, and willingness to become involved in group discussion and activity. Other probable changes will be far greater concentration powers and markedly original thinking. This kind of growth is apparent after four or five meetings; in some cases it occurs much sooner.

The time has come now for suggesting more complicated change-of-mood pantomimes to be developed with groups of related characters, rather than individuals, as has been done up to this time. Projects of this nature often require small groups of three or four to work together, in a corner of the room, prior to playing the scene. They will need to discuss the assignment, expand on their characters, plan for entrances and exits, and generally discuss new ideas to use in the improvisation. It is obvious that this kind of creative interaction cannot take place naturally and spontaneously until the seniors all feel reasonably secure and free from tension. Even when this is the case, the leader must observe closely and pick up quickly the slightest sign of timidity or withdrawal on the part of any participant. Should the four or five small group discussions bog down, it is the leader's prerogative to assist tactfully, by suggestion, until the planning is again on the track and moving forward. Every effort must be made to prevent any feeling of failure or inadequacy. The decision to progress to more complex material must be determined by the readiness and attitude of most of the group members.

5
From Dramatic Play to Drama

CHANGE-OF-MOOD PANTOMIME

As we move into change-of-mood pantomime we progress from *dramatic play* to *drama.* The single mood pantomime can last for ten seconds, ten minutes, or until the leader gives a cue for its conclusion. For example: the lady whom we introduced in Chapter 4, who was disappointed over not receiving her grandson's birthday greeting card, might walk from the post office, a few feet, or a half a mile. There is no indication of a stopping place for the action or a limitation of time set by the story form. By suggesting, in the earlier chapter, that the end of the room become "home," we automatically gave the scene a time and space limit. Let us consider, now, what would happen to such an exercise, if supplemented to become a change-of-mood pantomime. Suppose that as the grandmother walks sadly along, she hears her name called. She turns to see a postman coming to give her the long-awaited card, sent special delivery. Her mood changes to excitement and anticipation as she hurries joyfully to her destination, card in hand. This mini-scene has a beginning, a climax, and a denouement (here, a "they-all-lived-happily-ever-after" fairy tale ending). The mood changes have given the scene dramatic form. Dramatizing this kind of material is more interesting, more fun, and also more difficult, because it demands a great deal of concentration and a variety of thought patterns.

A scene involving a related group of three or four characters can provide a natural and valuable preparation for work in improvised dialogue which is soon to follow. This kind of dramatization, concerning a few friends or family members, presents several new problems. We have already noted that up to this time, although six or eight have been playing at the same time, they have worked as individuals, not a related group. One might say that they have been working *in* a group but not *as* a group. What one thought was not affected by the behavior of the others. Each person could finish his story in his own time. Now, in pantomiming change-of-mood group scenes, the participants will be playing as a closely related group. Any incident or thought change on the part of one character may influence the behavior of the others. Spontaneous reaction and interaction is vital to the flow of the drama. It is, therefore, essential that every detail of the story and the appearance of the setting be explicit and thoroughly understood. If there is a door or gate involved, disaster can result if two of the four players fail to use the door space indicated, but seem to go through the wall instead. Such errors, due to misunderstanding of the directions or the vagueness of the leader in explaining the scene, can seriously handicap the progress of a group of seniors. Some might be so upset over the failure to visualize the playing area correctly, that they will hesitate to volunteer to play the next assignment.

It is advisable at this stage to discuss again how feelings change. There is always a specific reason for every change of mood. It is easy to clarify this explanation by examining the imaginary sequence of events in a typical day of one's life. For example: One might arise on a dismal, rainy morning, anxious over an early appointment with the doctor. A phone call from a good friend, offering transportation may bring temporary relief and lift the spirit. Then, perhaps, after waiting for a friend for a half hour, even greater anxiety occurs, with thoughts of the doctor's rigid adherence to his appointment schedule. And so it goes, for most of us all day long. Events, bits of news, or a phone call change one's point of view. But always there is a reason for that mood change. The lesson implied here cannot be over-emphasized.

Since often the small group of three to five is expected to react as a unit, the leader may face a new problem, the solution of which lies in his hands alone. In a situation where a sound must be heard by all, in order to motivate a mood change, the leader must himself produce that sound (or some agreed upon sound) in order to synchronize the reactions. For example: A group of hikers have left their base camp to explore a newly-blazed trail. As darkness begins to fall, they realize that they are lost and unable to find the path by which they climbed the mountain. As they search in vain for the trail, becoming more and more disturbed, the faint sound of a human voice, calling, comes from a distance. All the players must hear this sound at exactly the same time. They will then stop to listen, thinking, What's that? Someone's calling! It is important that the leader make this sound, like a muffled call. When it is over, all is quiet; confusion may again take over. Another call comes, this one louder and perhaps close enough to be recognized. It is the camp director who has come to look for the wanderers. They soon see the glow of his flashlight waving in greeting. In great relief they go off to meet him. Without the leader's assistance, the sound of the rescuer could not motivate all players simultaneously and the group could not work as a unit. Should a creative musician be available to provide mood music for this kind of pantomime, change in the music, alone, can effectively indicate a sound cue.

It may prove helpful in developing confidence to ask some general questions prior to the playing of the story. This procedure will bring important incidents into sharp focus, and suggest details and thought sequences which will facilitate the dramatization. The leader might ask, for example, "What would you be thinking as it begins to get dark and you can't locate the trail back to camp?" Spontaneous responses will come back, such as, What are we going to do? We're lost! We can't spend the night up here. What'll we do for food? Will they miss us at the camp? This is so frightening! The leader accepts these thought ideas, perhaps adds several of his own, and then proceeds, "And when we hear that far off voice for the first time, does our thinking change?" More replies will be forthcoming at once. By the time each section of the story, with its changing moods, has been closely examined, the players will begin to feel more and more secure, relaxed and ready.

However, before any attempt at dramatization is made, a review of the appearance of the imaginary forest scene is advisable. Everyone must know what is to be included. Are there tall trees, scrub and underbrush? Are there rocks or tree stumps where one might sit? And where will the voice and light come from? In what direction will we go to answer the rescuer's call? To some leaders this detailed planning and discussion may seem unnecessary and superfluous. Experience has proven, however, that it is absolutely vital to success in a senior group! Only when each individual feels very sure of the plot line, the imaginary place in which the action occurs, as well as the exact sequence of the thought patterns, can he feel free from tension and comfortable enough to enjoy participation. He needs also to be assured that although all players are reacting to a common experience, each is an individual and will have a different response to any given circumstance.

SELECTING MATERIAL

The selection of material for change-of-mood pantomime should present no problems. The field is broad, almost unlimited; one can draw from the whole of life and its varied human relationships. A few specific guidelines which may prove helpful follow:

1. The situation chosen should be within the interest and experience range of the participating seniors. (i.e., a scene concerning children or teenagers would not be appealing or believable, while a city-oriented group might have difficulty identifying with rural or farm problems.)

2. The story should be dramatic in form, including the initial incident of an implied conflict, action which rises to a climax, and a satisfactory conclusion; more simply stated, it should have a beginning, a middle, and an end.

3. The problem to be solved in the mini-conflict should concern and appeal to the average senior. When he can completely identify with a character, he can more readily recreate such a person's thoughts and feelings.

4. Incidents concerning human relationships which offer opportunities for discussion of ethical standards and fine philosophies are recommended. In my opinion, this applies to material for all age groups, and it is particularly important for the seniors, most of whom have grown to honor and cherish the good things of life: compassion, love, generosity, sharing, self-sacrifice, and courage.

5. The sources of ideas are many. Dramatic real life stories often appear in current magazines and newspapers. Sometimes poems, such as Edwin Markham's "The Right Kind of People," can suggest moving relationships especially for dialogue scenes. Often the members themselves will bring a real experience to the group, which can be easily adapted for playing.

6. One last note concerning selection of material for dramatization could almost be considered a warning. The temptation to use superficial or comic situations should be resisted. Believable dramatization of good comedy is extremely difficult. Such attempts by seniors may end in

overdone clowning to stimulate laughter. Often this becomes "laughing at" rather than "laughing with." Little growth and many hurt feelings may result, for despite their denials, older adults do *not* enjoy being the butt of a joke.

Some examples of material successfully used in our groups are included here. If they do not seem appropriate for another leader's sessions, they may serve as models for other situations which he may develop to meet his needs more adequately. I feel compelled to offer a last word of advice which applies to introducing the material for pantomime or dialogue improvisation. *First,* prepare the story carefully. The original material may need to be revised and changed to suit the needs of a particular group; characters may be added, or eliminated, the age of those involved may need to be different; several incidents may work more effectively if they occur in the same place rather than in different scenes. This homework, done conscientiously, will save much valuable class time and will keep the interest high. *Second,* tell the story dramatically, with genuine enthusiasm, using direct discourse whenever possible. Above all, enjoy it! If the leader finds it exciting to tell, the group will find it exciting to play.

Dramatic Situations

1. Marge and Elizabeth, twin sisters, and Alice, their good friend, plan to spend their sixty-fifth birthday at the home of Jean, Marge's daughter. This is a great place for a party since there are three grandchildren who will surely participate. The scene opens on an empty stage. The three enter, coming in from a shopping trip a little early. Suddenly, through the half-open door of an adjacent room, come the excited voices of the grandchildren, discussing their plans for the surprise. The ladies, as they listen, realize that they must somehow get out so they will not spoil the grandchildren's plans. Very quietly, on tiptoe, they move back

toward the street door, deciding they will walk a bit in the park and come back later.

2. Three friends have gathered in the kitchen of a mountain cottage where they are spending a summer vacation. One has put a cake in the oven. As she finishes washing up the bowl, she glances in the oven and is satisfied that the cake is fine. Another is helping a third to find a jig-saw puzzle which together they dump out on a center table. The "cake-baker" joins them and they start to work. They get so involved in the puzzle that they forget the cake entirely. Suddenly one thinks she smells something burning. She rises, goes to the oven as she remembers the cake. The others watch, very troubled. And they have reason to be worried! The baker takes the cake out and finds the edges are impossibly burned! The smell is so unpleasant that one friend opens the door and they take the cake outside to the garbage can. (Note: Before playing this scene, the rules must be designated carefully. Who will make the cake? Who will get out the puzzle? Which one will first smell the burning cake? Who will take it from the oven? Who will open the door? The placement, too, of table, oven, sink, door, etc. must be agreed upon by all players.)

3. Two (or three) older people are staying with the grandchild of one, in the young parents' place in an area about ten miles from a small town. The young couple have gone to a concert being given in town, a rare occasion for them. Grandmother and her friend(s) have come to baby-sit with the little one, who is asleep upstairs. The older folks may be knitting, reading, watching and feeding the open fire, or listening to music. Suddenly there is a small scratching sound. Only one hears the noise. Then it comes again, louder; they are all aware, and a little frightened! As they all finally locate it coming from the direction of the front door, the first to hear it decides to investigate. The

others, more apprehensive, try to stop her but she proceeds valiantly. Cautiously, she opens the door a crack and then, almost immediately, all the way. There, on the threshold, is a tiny, lost, shivering little puppy, wet from the rain and begging for shelter. They are all greatly relieved and sympathetic, too, as the first lady picks up the puppy and proceeds to the rug in front of the fire. Another goes for a towel to dry him off, and a third comes forward with a biscuit for the shaking little animal. Together they get him comfortable on the rug by the fire and then go back to their occupations, knitting, reading, etc. just as we found them at the beginning.

4. In Chapter 3, we suggested that some vagabonds on a journey, one hot day, might enter a prolific apple orchard, surrounding a seemingly deserted house, to gather some fruit. The same basic story can be adapted for a change-of-mood situation. As the trespassers gather apples, they might hear a door of the house slam, and see, through the old trees, the gardener coming down the steps. Guiltily they each dash for the nearest hiding place, an old shed, a tree, some shrubbery. Finally, when they see him go back up the steps and into the house, they creep carefully over to the old gate and out of the orchard to safety.

5. You are visiting cousins who live in the lowlands very close to the Mississippi River. A series of rain-filled days has swelled the river to the flood stage. The grounds of the little cottage are all under water and you have been warned by the state police to be prepared for evacuation in the morning unless the rains stop and the water recedes. When our scene opens all three (or four) are asleep in sleeping bags, comfortable chairs and on the floor. The sound of the bell from the village church wakes everyone. Remembering the police warning of the night before, all listen, fearfully, wondering whether the rain has stopped.

Finally one gets the courage to rise and move toward the curtained window. The others hardly dare stir! Number one pushes the heavy curtains aside, and as she does, a beam of sunlight shines in. The others go to the window; they can hardly believe what they see. The water is actually receding perceptibly. They embrace each other with joy, or perhaps silently say a prayer of thanksgiving, and then run off to notify the others that they are safe.

6. You and a friend are sitting on a beautiful beach, on a lovely day, drinking in the beauty of the blue sky and the sapphire sea. You have waited a long time for this vacation and it is all you could have hoped for. You both are so absorbed in the silent, peaceful beauty of it all that neither has noticed a group of young lads who have started to play with a beach ball higher up on the sand behind you. All-of-a-sudden, your friend cries: "Look out! Look out for the ball!" and you duck your head just in time to avoid the beach ball which seemed to be aimed directly at you. Fortunately, it didn't even graze your shoulder; in relief you watch the teenage offender run past to retrieve the ball from the edge of the ocean, calling an apology as he dashes by. Deciding to look for a safer spot, you and your friend rise and walk on down the beach. (Note: In this exercise the leader must give the cue: "Look out for the ball!")

7. (Note: This last exercise is somewhat more demanding and should only be attempted when the group is feeling secure and comfortable working together.) Pass along to six captains of six groups of three, three separate envelopes; ask the captains to draw one slip from each envelope. One packet will contain seven or eight slips on which are written "mood words," such as *Anger, Suspicion, Sadness, Fear, Happiness, Boredom.* In another packet the slips contain "place words" like *Attic, Cellar, Airport, Garden, Hotel, Lobby, Forest, Office.* On the slips in the third envelope,

are "object words," *Ring, Letter, Hat, Newspaper, Box, Book, Flashlight.* Each captain will now take his group to a corner of the room where they can discuss the three words selected on which they will build a mood pantomime in which all three will play. For example: one captain has selected 1) *Attic,* 2) *Suspicion,* and 3) *Ring.* Someone suggests that perhaps a ring has been lost or apparently disappeared. Another may add that a visiting niece is suspected of borrowing it to wear to a ball. Eventually the discussion will culminate in this story. Two widowed sisters live now with an old friend in a college town, where the husband of one had taught for many years. A niece has come to stay for the weekend to attend a prom at the college. The friend, in discussing the amethyst ring her mother left her, goes to the drawer to get it to show it to the two sisters. The box has disappeared. The two sisters very much resent the fact that their friend seems to suggest that the young woman, who knows about the ring, has borrowed it to wear to the prom. They suggest that they look in several boxes in the attic where their hostess usually keeps her old letters and jewelry. The scene begins when the three enter the attic, and look about for the several old chests where the treasures are kept. One of the sisters (designated beforehand) discovers the box holding the ring inside one of the chests. She shows it to the others in great glee, almost with an "I told you so!" attitude. The three, in great relief, leave the attic, taking the ring with them. (This story played extremely well, and is a good example of satisfactory creative interaction in a small group of seniors. Their time for preparation was approximately ten minutes.)

GUIDES FOR PROSPECTIVE LEADERS

As I conclude these suggestions for change-of-mood pantomime, I feel disposed to review some of the indispensable practices for the prospective leader. Since most of these thoughts apply as well to work with original dialogue, with which we will deal in Chapter 6, reflecting on them now will be especially advantageous.

1. The group must *all* see clearly the physical aspects of the scene—entrances, exits, doors, windows, furniture placement, and the like.

2. Everyone must understand the whole story, character relationships, and at what point the actual playing begins.

3. One must have a specific reason for every change of mood and every changing thought. Telling one's self, Now I must be angry (or sad), will never produce believable action.

4. When the whole group needs to react to the same sound, the leader must be responsible for giving the cue. He should explain, before the playing, exactly what the cue will be so the sound will be expected and will not break the concentration.

5. When necessary, individual players should be assigned certain specific duties to keep the scene moving forward. For example, in Exercise 3, one should be designated to hear the scratching sound first, one must get the towel, another pick up the dog, and so on. This preparation will avoid confusion and keep the action smooth.

6. Although many leaders tend to shy away from serious material which calls forth deep feelings, I heartily recommend it. In life, our most moving experiences are associated with sorrow and joy. Improvisations in this area can develop imaginative understanding of how to sustain one's self in sadness and even personal bereavement. It can also make us more sensitive and understanding of others during their difficult times.

6
Beginning to Use Dialogue

Only the perceptive, sensitive leader can decide when his group is ready to communicate in words. Friendliness, spontaneous conversation, and relaxation are good signs. When bodies seem to be reacting freely with good coordination, when imaginations have been activated and pantomimes are believable, the moment for introducing work with speech has probably arrived. Despite such signs of readiness, taking this forward step is likely to present some problems with any senior group. Because many of them live in isolated conditions, the opportunities to converse freely are few. Sometimes, when they do manage to express their own ideas, the response is hostile or impatient, often increasing their sense of insecurity and inadequacy. As a result, many older people have practiced restraint or silence simply in self-defense.

Up to this point, all of our exercises have required that thoughts and feelings be communicated in action alone. The first efforts to verbalize them may seem difficult or even frightening to some. The very sound of one's own voice, in improvised speech, brings with it a certain shock. Merely because of the lack of daily practice, putting the right words together to express a thought seems an impossible task. As leaders, we must be prepared for this kind of behavior, be relaxed and patient and start very simply. We should never expect marked success at the beginning.

Some introductory remarks, reviewing the relationship of body movement to physical and emotional changes, will be helpful. It should soon become apparent that the same factors influence changes in the quality and pitch of the voice. Strong emotions like anger, fear, hatred, and suspicion can readily be recognized in the sound of one's voice, as can the gentler emotions of compassion, joy, anticipation, sympathy. The two *KEYS* mentioned many times as basic to success in pantomime, are even more significant in dialogue exercises. Another related point to be emphasized at this time is that all new feelings and thoughts enter the heart and mind through one of the senses. One sees, hears, touches, tastes, or smells something, thus initiating a new thought pattern and a different mood. Speech, then, becomes a three-step procedure: (1) one sees (hears, touches, tastes, smells); (2) one thinks thoughts suggested by the sense experience; and (3) one speaks these thoughts aloud.

A demonstration of this theory is advisable. The leader may say, "I'm exploring a most interesting tropical forest." (At this point he looks up as though spying an unusual brightly-colored bird flying from tree to tree.) "Look!" (He says this in an obviously excited manner). The following questions, posed to the seniors, usually bring eager, spontaneous responses, What did I see? Was it exciting? Have I ever seen such a thing before? They will guess that there was some unusual animal or bird in the trees; they will notice that the experience is pleasing and exciting. And they will realize that the one word, "Look" has told them everything. The need for the three-step procedure rule will be clear at once. The leader has (1) *seen* the bird; (2) *thought,* How interesting! How exciting! and then (3) *spoken* aloud the word "Look!"

As we initiate work with dialogue, another problem must be kept in mind. During the early classes, groups of a half dozen or more have worked together; at the very start, the simple activity pantomimes used the entire class. There was little chance for any feeling of self-consciousness. Now, the opposite is true. The first dialogue exercises should include only two or three. Improvisations with six or eight people can only end in chaos and may be very discouraging for those involved. This happens because some seniors, who are less secure, will wait for others to begin to speak; others, who have ideas, may talk at once, eager to make some contributions to the scene. In either case, the efforts can only meet with failure. A beginning which has proven very successful is the use of single words as practice material. The word "Look!" or a similar exclamatory phrase, as suggested in the earlier demonstration, can be used in many interesting ways. The leader can place two chairs a few feet apart, designating the space between as "the open door of your room." "Now, let's imagine," he will say, "that you are returning to your room after being out all day. Something about it has changed while you were away. There is something new or different about it, a change in appearance, a box on the floor; there is disorder here, perhaps, or a bunch of beautiful flowers, a letter or even a person whom you don't expect to find here. When you discover the change, just say one word like 'Look!' or a similar exclamation. We will see if we can guess what has happened, just by the sound of your voice. And remember the procedure has three steps: *Look, Think, Speak.*"

Although it is true that only one person can speak at a time, there will not necessarily be a feeling of self-consciousness if four or five can line up together about ten feet from the imaginary door and approach the open space one at a time. This arrangement will keep anyone from feeling that he is working alone. The critique period may be a bit easier to handle if each player has one observer assigned to watch him, to discuss what he found in his room and what mood the discovery motivated. The same kind of situation can be used with the word "Gone." Several specific incidents follow which may be used by the players with this word. If, on the

Three different reactions resulting from the dialogue exercise discussed on the page opposite. The participants, returning home to their rooms after being out all day, were asked to imagine that something had been changed and then to express their reactions with gesture and some verbal exclamation. Photographs by William L. Klender. Courtesy of the author.

other hand, they wish to create their own circumstance, so much the better. In each of these cases, only the word "Gone" is spoken.

1. I open the door of my sister's apartment, where we were supposed to meet. She isn't there!
2. I look in my jewelry box for a diamond necklace which I plan to wear to the concert. The box is empty.
3. I watch the last remnants of the old school, where I spent such happy days, being demolished for the building of a highway.

It will be obvious at once how important the first *KEY* is (make a picture in the mind) to the above scenes. One must see the picture in his mind's eye, if his verbal response is to be convincing.

By this time, it is to be hoped that self-confidence will have increased and people will be ready to volunteer to experiment with more speech. Some of the other single words which have been successfully tested as motivators are: *Mine, At last, Hello, No, Forever, Wait.* It is helpful to list the words on the blackboard, and discuss many different circumstances in which one might imagine using any of them. Every leader is surprised at the imagination of the average senior in carrying out this assignment. One member of a class gave three extremely interesting ideas for the use of the word "Mine." (We agreed that it could become "It's mine" or "That's mine.")

1. I have left a reference book which I have been using in the public library on a table while I go to the bookshelf. A young man suddenly picks up the book and goes off with it to the other side of the room. I say *(angrily),* "That's mine!"
2. Friends have been helping me to search for an antique earring which I have dropped at a reception. One discovers it, broken, and brings the pieces to me. I accept it, saying *(sadly),* "It's mine."

3. A neighbor whom I scarcely know rings my doorbell and hands me a letter which went to her by mistake. I can hardly believe it; our mailman knows me so well. I take it, saying *(questioningly),* "Mine?"

Once more it is necessary to have these little scenes played individually, because no concentration is possible if several voices, using the same word, speak simultaneously. As others volunteer to develop scenes based on the single word assignments, the leader must remind them again, that only if one imagines a very specific situation, and thinks all of the appropriate thoughts, will the speech be convincing and believable. It is advisable to assign one person to watch each player, so that the incident enacted may be more completely discussed. Should the observer be unable to guess the scene played, the wise leader will step into the discussion to save any hurt feelings resulting from a sense of failure.

Another exercise, using only the words "Come in!" has proved interesting and successful. It does, however, make some demands upon the leader's spontaneity and imagination. He will introduce it this way: "I am coming around to call on several of you" (indicating a group of four or five). "You are each sitting in your own living room, near the front door, which has a small pane of glass near the eye level, so that you can see anyone who approaches. You may be reading, knitting, sewing, anything you like. I will knock on the door, and you will rise, look through the glass to see who is there, open the door and say to me, 'Come in!' But, there is a problem! I do not know who I am until you speak. By the tone of your voice I will know whether I am a boring neighbor, a book salesman, a bill collector, or a long lost friend. You will each decide now, who I will be, for you! Remember, whoever I am, you must ask me to come in. And I must answer, in character, after I have discovered who I am by the sound of your voice and your general behavior." This is an interesting and imaginative exercise, because it is challenging but difficult for the leader; I suggest that he attempt no more than four or five "visits" at a time.

ATTEMPTING MORE COMPLEX
DIALOGUE IMPROVISATIONS

After trying a number of these simple scenes, most of the seniors will be ready for more complex group dialogue situations. One must remember, however, that a new skill will be needed: the ability to listen and then respond to one another. Conversation is a two-way street, not a monologue; concentrated listening is essential. It is wise to begin with scenes requiring only two to four characters. This is the direct opposite of the activity pantomime sessions where sometimes the whole class was used, and it poses a special problem. Even though only a few are involved, confusion is likely unless material requiring little dialogue is carefully selected and explained in great detail. The scenes should be told in direct discourse, as far as possible. As the characters seem to speak, during the telling of the story, they come alive. This facilitates their re-creation by the seniors.

One of the surest roads to success at the beginning is to return to some of the familiar situations used for mood and change-of-mood pantomime mentioned in Chapters 4 and 5. These incidents have already been thoroughly discussed; characters, story line and settings are old friends. There is great advantage in having this preliminary analysis, which must be accorded new material, already completed. Attention can now be focused on adapting the situation for communication, using speech as well as action. Some exercises may need an extra character, a slight change of place or time, and all should have a detailed review of the sequence of ideas to be used as the conversation proceeds.

All of the exercises in Chapter 5, numbers one through seven, listed under the heading "Dramatic Situations," beginning on page 64 can be so adapted. To understand this method more clearly, let us analyze the change-of-mood scene about the hikers who lose the newly-blazed trail some miles away from the base camp. The story line and setting have already been established; the groundwork has been laid. In order to sharpen memories, the leader might restate some of the thoughts, in greater detail. This procedure will furnish a generous supply of ideas to be used for the conversation. If three or four players are used, certain individuals must be given the responsibility of dealing with key points in the story: 1) the coming of darkness and the need to get back to the camp, 2) the lost trail, 3) the first distant sound of the rescuer's voice, and 4) the recognition of the director's voice and the comforting sight of his flashlight. The rest of the conversation, to which all contribute, will flesh out the bare bones of the plot and make the scene come alive.

It is often helpful for the leader to ask some definite questions before the playing begins, in order to focus on important ideas for the dialogue. For the present scene, he may ask, "What would the hikers be discussing at the opening of the scene?" A player might suggest, "The beauty of the spot and the ease in following the newly-blazed trail." Another might want to include something about those left behind, such as, "Won't the others at the camp be surprised to find that we made it so easily?" A perceptive player may say, "Then someone will have to notice that the sun has set and we'd better get back . . . and then we will start to look around for the trail."

Although none of these speeches may be used exactly as suggested, this group restructuring of the story will stimulate creativity and other original ideas will be forthcoming. It will help all of the participants to feel more confident about improvising dialogue, and an easy flow of the plot will be assured. Whatever the assignments in a single class, several groups should have a chance to play the same scene, following the detailed general discussion described above. A critique will follow each playing, and suggestions will usually be made about important bits of information omitted, or interesting lines, which, if added, could enrich the scene. The last group to play will have the advantage of having heard and absorbed ideas from the preceding critiques. Often those who have volunteered to begin will ask for a chance to play the scene again, in order to improve on their initial efforts. Unless interest seems to wane, the same scene can be repeated by all who want to avail themselves of the opportunity. This practice of analysis, discussion, and then replay is a significant factor in the growth and development of the seniors involved.

In like manner, the other six episodes suggested for change-of-mood pantomimes in Chapter 5 may be examined, adapted and, if necessary, revised for playing in dialogue. Besides using a complete story as exemplified in these scenes, the leader may vary assignments by suggesting more imaginative material for dialogue improvisation.

1. A group's designated captain may select from prepared envelopes (as used for change-of-mood pantomimes) an *object,* a *place,* and a *mood.* He will be given five or ten minutes alone with his players, during which they will develop a story line, characters and their relationships suggested by their three key words. They will plan the setting for the action and the general flow of conversation ideas. When they are ready, the captain will tell the observers his three key words and describe the setting which he has arranged with available chairs, stools, and the like. He may even mention the time of day, the time of year, the weather, or any other information which will set the mood for the playlet. In giving such an assignment, the leader must be sure that his group is ready for such a challenge. Individuals must feel free to interact, to accept or reject one another's ideas comfortably, and to create, in a limited

time, an imaginary situation which will be dramatic in
form. It is the leader's responsibility to observe the preparatory work carefully, to be sensitive to any group's need,
to step in and offer guidance where necessary, and to keep
the creative interaction progressing to a satisfactory conclusion.

2. A number of "character" faces may be clipped from
magazine advertisements and mounted on sheets of
brightly-colored construction paper. The sheets will be
numbered and spread out on an easily accessible long bench
or table. For this exercise, teams of three or four can be
used. Each team will be given a few minutes to examine the
"characters." They will agree on two or three whose
moods may suggest an incident which could be the basis for
an interesting scene. The group then withdraws to a
private section of the room, takes the five or ten minutes
allotted for developing the scene, and decides upon the
casting of characters involved, the setting, and the story
line. When they are ready, the captain makes the appropriate announcements to the observers and the playing begins.
This method of improvising is interesting but demanding;
only those who feel ready and willing should participate.

3. As the group progresses, a method calling for even more
spontaneous thinking might be used successfully. Again
the class should be divided into small workable groups of
three or four. From an envelope each captain will draw a
slip which contains a short description of the situation and
a first line to be said by the captain as he enters the scene.
His other players only know who and where they are, not
the line to be spoken. Example: One captain draws a slip
on which is written:

> You are members of the same family, who are waiting at
> an airport for another member whom you haven't seen
> for many years. One of your group comes into the scene
> and says: "He isn't coming. The flight's been canceled."

The captain will say only to his players, "We are all related, and we are waiting in an airport. I will come into the waiting room and speak to you. Our conversation will develop from this one line." As he enters and speaks, one player may ask the obvious question, Who's not coming? in order to establish some of the basic facts needed for the story to grow. Another might say, Why is the flight canceled? or Where was it coming from? or Can't he take the next flight? And gradually the interchange of ideas will give some form and unification to the scene; a possible story develops and continues to a satisfactory ending. Some amusing situations occur as the various participants must reply to unexpected questions.

4. An entirely different approach demands imaginative planning of a situation for which the dialogue only is given to two participants. The lines are written on small slips of paper. One volunteer selects a slip and a partner with whom he will create the scene. They are given a few minutes to work together to develop the action pattern. They may use as much pantomime as they wish preceding the dialogue, but only the words given. It is up to the two players not only to create the situation, but also to decide upon their individual characters and their relationship. We call this improvisation game "Couplets." Several workable bits of dialogue follow. (A & B designate the two characters involved.)

  (1) A—You've come back!
     B—Yes!

  (2) A—What time is it?
     B—Eleven o'clock.

  (3) A—Well?
     B—It's true.

  (4) A—You're going?
     B—Yes.

    (5) A—Hello!
        B—Hello!
        A—You're back?
        B—Yes.

Many unusual and varied circumstances can be developed from the same dialogue sequences. Let us take number one as an example. The situation might concern a mother and her unmarried daughter. The latter, feeling unhappy about having to assume so much responsibility for so many years, has finally run off, after a bitter argument. Realizing how she must have hurt her mother and also how miserable she will be alone, she returns to apologize. The scene opens with mother sitting in a rocker, knitting or reading. She hears footsteps, looks up expectantly. The daughter is standing silently in the doorway, ashamed, remorseful. The forgiving mother rises, reaches out welcoming arms and says, "You've come back!" The daughter runs to her and hides her face in the warm embrace as she murmurs, "Yes!" The same couplet might suggest, to another pair, a scene between a wife and her wayward, impetuous husband. He is always ending arguments with a threat to leave home unless he has his way. Somehow, like a bad penny, he always turns up again. In this case the wife's remark, as she looked up knowingly toward the opening door, would have an I-might-have-guessed-it tone. She might even have to add a word or two for emphasis, "So . . . you've come back!" He would respond sulkily as he sneaks off to his study, "Yes."

Many benefits are derived from these more complex improvisations. First, members of a group working together learn how to exchange ideas constructively, how to give and take. Second, the creative imagination is constantly challenged and motivated into action. Third, human understanding deepens as one becomes another character. Fourth, one's ability to express inner thoughts and feelings spontaneously and naturally is substantially increased. Fifth, one learns one of life's most important lessons—to listen as well as to speak.

William Bridge, a fine teacher, made an important statement many years ago about values integral to this kind of experience. He says, in part, in his *Handbook on Improvisation,* ". . . life consists of a sequence of impromptu situations, in which the individual acts with only a minimum of foresight. . . . In improvisational drama we project the individual into situations in which he must invent his way out . . . find new words and a new voice. . . ." Bridge feels that the player, under these circumstances, calls forth unexpressed factors of his personality and releases hidden psychic and emotional resources. This not only enriches his "experiencing self" but obliges him to invent and create constantly.

This exercising of imaginative powers and sharpening of sensitivities and responsiveness play a dynamic role in the senior's growth and change. After a number of sessions devoted to these dialogue exercises, remarkable development will be evident in most of the participants. Because they feel a new sense of well-being, the spirit and morale in the group is high; much has changed! The cliques, which were a problem in the beginning, don't exist; the withdrawn attitude of some of the more lonely members has disappeared; there is now no one who hesitates to contribute to the general critiques and discussions. They have been together only six or seven weeks and yet they have become good friends, caring about one another and openly sharing their thoughts and feelings. It is time now for the last and most difficult step, the actual playing in improvised dialogue of some longer, serious, and dramatic life situations, designed by the leader.

7
Improvisations Based on Life Experiences

The dialogue exercises of the previous weeks will have laid a firm foundation on which to create the small play. This is the last, most interesting, and most difficult kind of improvisation. Selecting material for such an activity with seniors is a ticklish undertaking, for even the most proficient leader; many things must be thoughtfully considered. The readiness and the ability of the group members come first; the socioeconomic background will also affect the choice. The story's theme and the nature of the characters play an important part in the success of the experiment. Unless the participants are interested in and sympathetic with the basic elements of the story, their response will be less than enthusiastic. Although the plot need not deal exclusively with people over sixty, it should concern characters and a dramatic conflict familiar to this age group. One can hardly expect seniors to develop believable characterizations of teenagers; they are likely to become merely caricatures. The material should ideally be based on life situations and problems with which seniors can easily identify. Conflicts suggesting several possible solutions will usually provoke interesting discussions, disclosing deep insight into human relationships. This involvement plays a very significant part in reaching some of our most important goals; sharpening sensitivity and awareness, deepening human understanding, and stirring compassion.

To summarize, we will be wise to consider the following guideposts in selecting material for playing the story:

1. In order to have real dramatic impact, the improvisation material must contain a conflict leading to a crisis or climax and then to an ending which solves the problem and releases tension.

2. Any playable situation should have strong human interest and emotional appeal.

3. The plot line should suggest action that moves directly to a high point with the possibility of a fast, satisfactory denouement.

4. A worthwhile theme is advantageous, as are consistent, believable, true-to-life characters.

5. Material of a somewhat serious nature is recommended. Discussions of well-rounded characters and their relationships deepen human understanding and touch the heart. Comic material, on the other hand, ·is likely to motivate only superficial comments and exhibitionist behavior in senior players, rather than increase their ability to express genuine emotion.

6. It is advisable to abide by the rules imposed by the "classic unities" of *time, place* and *action.* The story incidents should occur in sequence, in the same place, and within a continuous, limited time span.

Once the play material is selected, it must be carefully analyzed, adapted, and revised by the leader. He will prepare it for presentation to the group always with his own seniors in mind; the importance of this careful preparation cannot be over-emphasized. Telling the story in direct discourse will help it to come alive. Only if the leader is completely familiar and comfortable with the material can his enthusiasm color it with suspense and excitement. My dear friend, Geraldine Siks, beautifully describes the art of telling a story to be dramatized by a group of young people. The same suggestions apply here. She says, "To share a story creatively, a leader first makes the story her own . . . she reads it again for sheer enjoyment . . . edits and analyzes the story's moods and drama elements. . . . She sees it happening . . . unfolding, she identifies with the characters. A story must become real and alive to a leader before she can make it live for others."

The next procedure is analysis of the story, the characters, and the settings, initiated by the leader, but soon becoming a vital group discussion motivated by carefully phrased questions. A demonstration and guide for this procedure appears following the first recommended story in this chapter. This preparatory work may seen to consume a great deal of time; one can rest assured, however, that it will be a good investment.

It is especially important for the whole group to understand every detail of the story—the relationship of the characters and the movement of the plot—from the initial incident to the denouement. The appearance of the scene in which the action takes place must be agreed upon, the entrances and exits placed, and any real or imaginary properties discussed and provided for. Suggestions from members of the group should be accepted as often as possible. If they must be rejected, the leader will give convincing grounds for not accepting them, based on the required elements of good drama.

Once all these facts have been established, the class may be divided into small groups for developing the little play. The practice, recommended earlier, of having several groups work on the same material is again advised. Observing and discussing different interpretations of the same story can spark original thinking and creativity, considering the variety of surprising but believable endings. This is comforting evidence of positive growth, increased self-confidence, and sincere, absorbed participation. These are encouraging signs of progress. The dramatic situations, explained in some detail at the end of this chapter, have all been used successfully with seniors. They are, however, intended only as examples to suggest ideas, not to place any limitation on the group leader's own originality. Since the needs of any group depend entirely on its composition, every leader will probably have to create much of his own material. Although characters in many of the exercises seem written for women, a little revision can easily adapt them for men.

Groups which make fast progress may be challenged after a dozen sessions by building their own stories for improvisation; three or four might work together over several class periods. One such senior project found a suggested list of incidents, places, and theme statements useful for this purpose. Four examples follow:

1. An incident occurring on a bus trip to the beach.
2. A jury is attempting to reach a difficult verdict.
3. A bus breaks down on a lonely mountain road.
4. An archaeologist and friends make an exciting discovery at a "dig" in Greece.

Another group found inspirational ideas in single lines, such as:

1. We should have gone the other way. I know we should.
2. Why didn't you phone the police?
3. Nobody will believe us, no matter what we say!
4. Look! It's ruined. She'll be furious.

In all of these cases, the theme, place or single line merely serve as catalyst for creativity. From the combined group thinking, a dramatic conflict, the characters, the story line, and an appropriate ending emerge. This method of story improvisation is obviously much more challenging and is only successful with an eager, advanced group. If, however, seniors can successfully develop their own play program in this manner, the rewards and satisfactions are enormous. Invaluable personal benefits are derived from the experience of group interaction, and from the discipline imposed by the need to give and take constructive criticism and to build selflessly toward the unity of the play project.

Stories for Improvisation

The following five stories are told in some detail. A suggestion for the number of roles, male and female characters, has been made, but this is subject to change. A general description of the setting is included. To facilitate matters, abbreviations for stage terms have been used: stage right—S.R., stage left—S.L., upstage—U.S., and down stage—D.S. (With apologies to those readers who are experienced in theatre, I explain: Left and right refer to the actor's left and right; upstage means the back of the acting area; downstage the front section.)

1.   *REJECTION*

A story of the unhappy consequences of prejudice. Three characters (female).

Characters

MARGE ⎫
JEAN ⎬ two old friends
KIM, a Korean girl

Scene

A college dormitory, the living room in a two-room suite. Besides several pieces of casual furniture there must be a daybed, or couch U.S. center, a door to the hall D.S.L. and a door to the inner bedroom, D.S.R., which is partly open. At rise, the stage is empty. There is a suitcase of some foreign origin, with tags indicating Korea, on the floor, near center stage.

Marge and Jean are in their early sixties, old friends, fairly affluent, and happy over their decision to go back to school at a nearby college to finish work on their graduate degrees. They are delighted that despite the popularity of this institution, they have been able to get the suite of rooms they wanted, even though their application was late. Their voices can be heard as they come down the hall toward the suite; they are obviously concerned and angry.

MARGE: *(off)* How would such a reputable institution dare do this to us? I cannot understand it.

JEAN: *(off)* Nor can I! It seems to me that we are paying enough for this suite to be permitted to occupy it alone.

MARGE: *(as they appear on stage)* And we paid in advance for the whole semester, which wasn't even required!

JEAN: That dean knew her request was absurd! She could hardly get the words out!

MARGE: Well, I'm not surprised! It was brazen of her to ask us to share this suite! Such things are just not done!

JEAN: And with a foreign student at that, a Korean woman! Imagine!

MARGE: And just because she's here sponsored by the Friends Service Committee, and struggling to do her final work on her law degree, we're suppose to be sympathetic enough to permit her to sleep in our living room! I think . . . *(she sees the suitcase)* Well . . . she's moved in already! There's her suitcase! *(They examine it and improvise conversation about the tags, etc.)*

JEAN: *(leading the way into the bedroom through door at D.S.R.)* It's preposterous, that's what it is! Let's put our bags down and then go to see the dean! *(as they disappear, leaving the door D.S.R. ajar,* KIM, *the Korean girl, comes in through the hall door at D.S.L. her eyes wide with wonder! At last her dream will come true! She smiles as she takes in the beautiful room and recognizes her suitcase. She is bursting with joy! Suddenly, she hears the conversation which begins again in the next room. More remarks concerning the unfairness of having to share with a foreigner, "an Oriental at that," and similar insulting inferences reach* KIM's *ears. She is stunned, deeply hurt, almost incredulous. Finally, realizing that she cannot stay where she is so unwelcome, she makes a decision, crosses to her suitcase, picks it up, and trying to hold back tears, leaves the room. Conversation from* MARGE *and* JEAN *informs us that they are preparing to go to complain to the dean. They enter from the bedroom door, at D.S.R.)*

MARGE: *(seeing the suitcase has disappeared)* Jean, look! It's gone! The suitcase has disappeared! Do you suppose . . .?

JEAN: Yes, she's been here. And she's gone, and taken the suitcase with her. She must have heard us. . . . Oh dear!

*   *   *   *   *

At this point, the leader might suggest that they decide what the ending will be. Through discussion, following some key questions as to how each character might feel, several closing lines may be suggested, and different reactions on the part of Marge and Jean. Groups of three may volunteer to develop the little play; they may each decide on their own ending, and ask for time to discuss their plans. A few minutes will be granted to those who feel they need this time.

We promised, at the beginning of this chapter, to analyze the first suggested story, in order to demonstrate how such a class discussion might proceed. After the first telling, the leader might ask such questions as, What did you think of the story? How do you feel about Marge and Jean and what are they like as people? Are they both alike, one just as self-centered and prejudiced as the other, or wouldn't it be more interesting to have one of them more deeply touched by Kim's hurt than the other? Much interesting comment will likely pour forth here; it is the leader's job to listen, to help guide the ideas along constructive paths, and to urge all the seniors to participate in the conversation. She might ask, Can you understand how Kim would feel as she listened to her potential roommates talking about her? Turn the attention now to the setting; some might even help the leader to set up the room, using available chairs, stools, tables, and the like, so that everyone sees the same room and entrances and exits. This will help those who volunteer to perform to feel comfortable moving about in a setting they completely understand. The question of needs for hand properties will naturally arise next; the Korean girl's suitcase, it is agreed, must be placed before the scene opens. (Anyone's large pocketbook or shopping bag will do for the moment.)

Next should come a discussion about the content of the dialogue units. The leader will ask, What will Marge and Jean talk about as they come down the hall, before they enter? What do we, the audience, need to gather from this conversation? In the same way, the leader discusses, helping only where necessary, the meat of the dialogue before the ladies enter the bedroom, and why it is important to stop the conversation for a minute or two during Kim's entrance and her surveying of the room. She must have a chance to show her excitement and joy about her wonderful good fortune, so that we, the audience, can identify even more deeply with her later disappointment and hurt. Marge and Jean must know about when to start their dialogue in the bedroom and what it will include. They must also understand that their entrance into the living room must depend upon the timing of Kim's departure. These facts must be made clear, even though they may conflict with some spontaneous suggestions from the group. It is important that everyone understand that only stories containing the elements of good drama will play successfully; timing of entrances and exits is one of these.

Turning to a discussion of the ending, the leader may ask, How might this end? Will either have a change of heart? Will they go to find Kim to apologize and welcome her? Will they go to the dean's office? Will Marge try to persuade Jean, or vice versa? Any or all of these ideas offer suggestions for potential endings. Some seniors feel secure if the leader helps them decide on the whole scene; others prefer to discuss it and develop their own ending. In any event, this preparatory experience is absolutely essential.

The remaining stories will be given in scenario form, rather briefly; dialogue content will be suggested rather than spelled out. It is hoped that the detailed presentation of the first story will be sufficient to guide the leader's preparatory session with the other scenes.

2. *THE TRIP*

A story involving personal sacrifice. A difficult decision must be made about giving up a much anticipated adventure. Three characters (two male, one female).

Characters

JIM ⎫
PETER ⎬ brothers, in their sixties

NANCY, their sister, in her seventies

Scene

The apartment where all three live. Peter and Jim, close in age, have had very different and somewhat difficult lives. But always there has been in the background the wise and loving sister, Nancy, who has often played the mother-advisor role and whom they both depend on and adore. Peter, who has never married, has lived most of his life with Nancy; Jim has had a disastrous marriage and has been with the other two only since the accident which destroyed his own family existence. Both men have worked hard and deeply appreciate

Nancy's help and guidance during the past ten years. Now, finally, better times have come, and the brothers have asked for vacation time together and have planned a trip to London, something they have looked forward to for years. Nancy, knowing that the trip is only two days away, has never told her brothers that she has had a series of trips to the doctor's office recently. She doesn't want to dampen their high spirits.

When the scene opens, the stage is empty. Soon we hear a key in the lock. Nancy enters from S.L., moving slowly, looking troubled, and holding a crumpled piece of paper in her hand. She goes to a table (center stage) and sits down, looking almost stunned, as she rereads the doctor's note which she is carrying. It contains the results of some recent tests and states that she must enter the hospital at the end of the week to undergo an operation. The news couldn't have come at a worse time. Suddenly, the telephone rings. Nancy, dropping the doctor's note on the table, goes quickly into her bedroom (offstage right) to answer the call.

In a moment we hear the men's voices, high in excitement, laughing as they joke about their last minute purchases. They enter at S.L., Jim puts his packages on a desk at U.R. and Peter drops his on the table at center. It is Peter who sees the crumpled note written on a doctor's prescription blank. Peter examines it, shocked. Jim, seeing Peter's consternation, stops in the middle of a sentence and goes to question him. Peter reads the unhappy news aloud. They are in a quandary! Their discussion, once the first shock is over, concerns the future, the trip. Shall they go or stay? Can they get a refund on tickets at this late date? While they are deep in this discussion, Nancy comes into the room, discovers the letter in their hands.

* * * * *

The ending should depend upon the decision of each group of players who try the scene. Will the men insist that they *must* give up the trip? Will Nancy persuade them to go? What will be the reasons which both give to back up their statements? Who will win out? In trying to persuade them to go, Nancy might say that she can't recuperate as well if she knows they have given up this trip! She may offer to call cousin Sue in Pittsburgh, who is a trained nurse, and ask her to come stay for two weeks. There are many possibilities for interesting and plausible endings. The various groups of three will enjoy developing their own conclusions.

3.   *MIXED CONNECTIONS*

Two grandparents, who have not been well, courageously fly to a foreign country to celebrate their granddaughter's sixteenth birthday. When there is not a familiar face at the airport, disaster threatens. Three characters (two females, one male).

Characters

ALICE THOMPSON } in their seventies
BEN THOMPSON
VIRGINIA BROWN, a friend of their daughter

Scene

The waiting room in an airport in Paris. There are several benches. An imaginary telephone is in a corridor, offstage right. Alice and Ben Thompson have spent most of their lives in a small, midwestern town. Peggy, their daughter, is married to a fine man, now in the foreign service in France. After much persuasion, the Thompsons have agreed to fly to Paris, where Peggy will meet them and drive them to her country house where daughter Patty's birthday will be celebrated. The action takes place in a quiet area near the TWA arrival desk, the agreed-upon meeting place. Alice is sitting on a bench looking miserable and frightened. Ben is pacing up and down, looking at his watch now and then.

After a minute or so the conversation begins.

ALICE: I just don't know what could have happened to Peggy, Ben. We've been here a half an hour. She's never late! And she must know we'll be scared to death in a foreign country like this.

BEN: I know, dear, I know! It does seem very strange—not like our Peggy at all!

ALICE: I'm worried, I really am! If something's happened to her, what can we do? We can't speak French, we couldn't even ask our way. Really Ben, I'm so frightened. I . . . *(she is on the verge of tears)*.

Ben tries to comfort Alice, giving any excuse he can think of for their daughter's unexplained absence. Finally, she asks if he remembered to put down her telephone number. He checks his wallet; yes, the number is there. Alice urges him to go off to the corridor (offstage right) where she has noticed a phone booth. He comes hurrying back to say that he forgot he only has American money. Alice saves this situation by producing some French change she had procured at the bank before they left home. Ben goes off again, and Alice paces nervously up and down. In a minute or so, Ben returns to say that there is no answer. Once more he tries to comfort Alice.

In the midst of this, a lady enters from S.L.; she is hurrying, looking about anxiously. Finally she approaches the couple and asks in English if they are the Thompsons, Peggy Carter's parents. They greet her warmly, and hasten to ask about Peggy. The newcomer, introduces herself as Virginia Brown, a friend and neighbor. She assures them that Peggy is in fine health and sends all sorts of apologies. Her car would not start this morning and the mechanic, who was late arriving, is still there trying to repair it. Mrs. Brown offers to drive them home and with great relief and much gratitude they gather up the bags and exit at S.L.

Workshop participants acting out story improvisations sketched out and discussed beforehand. Both scenes are from a Creative Drama workshop conducted by Rhoda Feuer. Photographs by Terry Buchalter. Courtesy of Brookdale Drama Project, directed by Milton Polsky.

4.   *THE BIG SWITCH*

A near tragedy caused by the mishandling of a luggage problem. Four characters (three females, one male).

Characters

MARGE ⎫
            ⎬ two friends
GRACE ⎭
JANET
THE DESK CLERK

Scene

A hotel lobby. There is a desk for registration purposes at S.L., a door leading to the street at D.S.R. and a door leading to elevators to the upper floors at U.S.R. There are several benches, or chairs, typical of those to be found in such public places. At rise, the hotel clerk is standing back of the desk, writing. Several suitcases stand on the floor near the desk. Two friends, Marge and Grace, enter through the D.S.R. door, talking about the trip.

MARGE: Well, it was a great flight and I'm so glad, especially for you, dear, with that big speech to make tonight.

GRACE: Yes, I must say, flying is not one of my favorite pastimes and it is important that I feel my best when I must speak on such a controversial subject right at the opening of the convention.

MARGE: You'll do a great job, dear. After all, you know your subject backward and forward and with that beautiful new dress, you'll be a big hit.

GRACE: I hope it traveled well. There'll never be time to get it pressed before the dinner—I'm sure of that. *(By this time they have reached the desk, speak to* THE DESK CLERK, *give their names, and sign the register as he gets out the reservation cards and assigns them rooms. Then he points to the bags which the limousine driver has already placed by the desk. Horrified,* GRACE *speaks.)*

GRACE: That's not my bag! But that's yours, Marge, isn't it?

MARGE: Yes! But they were both together at the airport! I don't understand!

Grace is beside herself as she tries to tell the clerk that she simply must have her own bag. All her notes for her very important speech are in her bag, not to mention her clothes and everything she needs for this important meeting. The clerk offers to look over at the baggage check point, near the door; he comes back empty-handed. There is more argumentative conversation which is finally interrupted by the entrance of another lady, Janet, who enters from U.S.R. carrying a bag very similar to the one on the floor by the desk. She comes to the desk clerk, furiously explaining that the wrong bag has been sent to her room. Marge, who is trying to comfort Grace as she sits disconsolately on a bench nearby, suddenly sees the bag and recognizes it as the one Grace has lost. There is a scurrying and finally agreement that the two bags, both of which were taken out of the airport limousine, must have been switched by mistake. After apologies all around, and much relief generally, the scene closes with the three ladies going off with their respective bags through the U.S.R. doorway and the desk clerk leaning on the counter, thankful that the irate ladies have finally been pacified.

* * * * *

5. *THE RIGHT KIND OF PEOPLE.*

This is the title of a poem by Edwin Markham. The theme provides a splendid base for a short play. The entire poem follows here and then a play originated by several of our seniors. Three characters (male).

Gone is the city, gone the day, yet still the story and the meaning stay:

Once where a prophet in the palm shade basked, a traveller
chanced, at noon, to rest his mules.
"What sort of people may they be," he asked, "in this
proud city o'er the plains outspread?"
"Well, friend, what sort of people whence you came?" the
prophet asked.
"What sort?" the packman scowled! "Why knaves and
fools," he said.
"You'll find the people here the same," the wise man said.
Another stranger in the dusk drew near and pausing, cried,
"What sort of people there in yon bright city, where the
towers rise?"
"Well, friend, what sort of people whence you came?" the
prophet asked.
"Oh! Good,—and true,—and wise!" the man replied.
"You'll find the people here the same,—the same." the
wise man said, and smiled!

Characters

PEDRO, a fisherman
FIRST TRAVELER
SECOND TRAVELER

Scene

An isolated rocky point of land in Spain, near a spot where
there is excellent fishing. A lovely village lies near the base of
the rocks. At rise, a wise old fisherman, native to these parts,
sits in the dusk mending his nets and watching the sea. He
looks up on hearing the sound of a motor nearby, and then
the steps of a tourist coming down the path. The man looks
disturbed, impatient as he speaks to Pedro, the fisherman.

FIRST TRAVELER: Good evening. Live around here?

PEDRO: Yes . . . for many years, friend. Can I help you?

FIRST TRAVELER: I hope so—I'm lost! Dreadful roads, no
signs—nothing! Got to stop for the night. What sort of
people live down in that village there?

PEDRO: Well, what sort of people live where you come from in America?

FIRST TRAVELER: Mostly a bunch of fools and greedy idiots, but that's true everywhere. Can't find anything else these days.

PEDRO: Well, friend, I guess you'll find the people here the same!

FIRST TRAVELER: Might have known it! Nothin' but bums in the world . . . that's all . . . Well! So long! *(He goes out to his car. The motor starts again, and* PEDRO *shakes his head, pitying the* TRAVELER*! He goes back to his nets.)*

SECOND TRAVELER: *(Coming quietly down the path, his knapsack on his back. He is obviously a hiker.)* Good evening, my friend—my fisherman friend, I should have said.

PEDRO: Good day, Sir! Yes, that's my trade, you guessed it. Have to get my nets mended before the morning.

SECOND TRAVELER: I'd like to help, but I'm not very good at such intricate work. I'm looking for a place to spend the night. Got to climb the mountain tomorrow early. What kind of people live there in that lovely village with the white church tower?

PEDRO: Well, friend, what sort of people are there in the town you come from?

SECOND TRAVELER: What sort? Let's see, most of them are good, and friendly, and wise and courageous. Great folks they are!

PEDRO: Hmm! Well, I believe you'll find the people here in my village just the same, my friend. And they'll have a warm welcome for you, I'm sure of that.

SECOND TRAVELER: Thanks friend, I'll go down then— before it gets too dark.

PEDRO: Good!*(Rising to show the way.)* The trail begins over there; it's a little steep in places, but you'll make it. Good evening, friend, happy traveling! *(He waves as the* SECOND TRAVELER *disappears, comes back to where his nets lie, smiling and delighted. He gathers his tools and his nets and follows the* TRAVELER *down the trail.)*

*　*　*　*　*

This beautiful poem can be dramatized in many ways, but more importantly, it provides food for deep thought and a lesson that many of us need to ponder on again and again: when one gives to others compassion, kindliness and love, he may expect ten-fold the amount in return.

Usually, during these sessions devoted to improvisation of simple stories, marked personality growth and change can be observed. Imaginations are more active; the ability to work together has increased appreciably; most participants will show great confidence in expressing themselves verbally. A genuine interest in observing the work of others and a facility in giving and accepting constructive criticism soon develops. Those who showed extreme reticence in the beginning are now enthusiastically entering into discussions about social and ethical problems suggested by the play material. Words like *openness, relaxation, joyous, enthusiasm, compassion* and *creative interaction* can be used to characterize the mood and attitude of every meeting.

8
Warm-Ups and Ice-Breakers

When sessions are convened only once a week, or even less frequently, it is advisable to begin the class with simple, game-like exercises. This kind of activity stirs the imagination, sharpens concentration powers, relieves tension, and prepares the way for the more complex work to follow. In addition, such warm-ups can usually be done with large groups or the whole class, thus energizing every member simultaneously. This is especially beneficial during the last half of the semester's sessions, when most of the dialogue projects are now assigned to small groups of three or four. This practice of involving everybody for a few minutes at the beginning stimulates interest in those who must later become observer-participants until it is their turn to perform. When this plan is not adopted, the members who are not called upon during the first half hour may become restless or inattentive during the first part of the class.

PANTOMIME EXERCISES FOR PARTNERED PAIRS

The following set of exercises will be most successful if the whole group is paired off into sets of partners, who are lettered rather than named, A and B. In other words, a group of twenty would have ten pairs of participants, an A and a B in each pair. If all the A's try an exercise and all the B's watch their respective partners, and then the procedure is reversed, the whole room can be active at one time. Partner B will

discuss or guess the meaning of partner A's pantomime and
then A will watch and discuss B's work. The leader must
guide all of the playing, giving cues for starting and finishing,
if necessary; it may be helpful if he makes some general
comments on the work before proceeding to the next exercise.

1. The A's will stand opposite their B partners, with about
   ten feet separating them. Partner A picks up an
   imaginary tennis ball, on cue, and starts a game of catch
   with his partner. On a signal from the leader—
   "Change!", the ball will become a basketball and the
   game will continue. The second time the leader calls
   "Change!" the ball will become a large beach ball. After
   another minute or two, the leader will give the signal to
   stop.

2. Each B will take a chair and place it about eight feet away
   from his A partner. The B's will then move about fifteen
   feet further away to their imaginary doors. Each will
   enter, in a very definite mood; something has happened to
   make him sad, angry, afraid, etc. He must think the
   thoughts appropriate to this incident and mood as he
   enters, closes the door, moves across the room to his
   chair, and sits down. His A partner will try to guess what
   has happened to him and to understand his mood when he
   enters. The game is then reversed—A and B change
   places. It is important that the leader remind the group
   that one *must* have a specific reason for feeling a certain
   mood; something must have happened to cause the
   feeling. Saying to one's self, Now I must act sad, will not
   elicit believable action. This may be done with the whole
   group or just five or six pairs; the other half may observe
   their colleagues' work.

3. Again the class will be organized into pairs, each A has a
   B partner. It is wise to change these partners frequently,
   so they will be working with different people for each

exercise. The A's will close their eyes, imagining themselves asleep in the early morning. The B's will watch them as they awake to the sound of an alarm clock cue given by the leader. The A's will rise, open a curtain near the bed, and discover torrents of rain. They will each have a definite reaction to the rain. It may discourage, disappoint, stir fear or joy or even disgust. The partner will watch his counterpart carefully as he reacts to the sight of the rain and then returns to his chair. In the critique period that follows, one at a time, the B's will comment on how the rain affected his partner's mood. The situation will then be reversed and the B's will open the curtain and discover the rain.

4. This exercise involves only the opening of a letter found on a table near an imaginary door. The addressee will enter, open and read the letter. His thoughts and feelings as he peruses it should show his partner what the letter contains. Is it good news, sad news, a frightening message, or perhaps an unintelligible one?

5. It is evening, at a lovely cottage in New England, beside a lake. You are walking slowly down to the end of the boat dock, taking a ring off your finger as you go. As you reach the end, make up your mind. Throw the ring into the deep blue-green water. Then walk back again to the cottage. One group will do this, their partners will observe closely and will guess the relationship of the performer to the ring. Why did he throw it away? What did the action mean in his life? This will be done by both groups.

6. This exercise is designed to develop concentration, awareness, and quick reaction. The A's line up on one side of the room, and the B partners stand directly in front of them; the lines are about three feet apart. One group is asked to be the players; their partners will be the reflections in a mirror. Any position taken by the player

must immediately be taken by his partner reflection. For example, if A as the player begins to move his right hand slowly over his head, then B as the reflection follows. Partner A then proceeds with the left hand, then with the head leaning to the right or to the left and so on. The reflection (B) must react instantly to take his player partner's positions. In other words, the B's must actually mirror the A's. At any moment the leader may say "Change!" The B's then become the players and the A's the mirrors.

7. Another game which challenges the powers of observation and concentration requires one group, let us say the A's, to observe carefully their partner B's appearance, the clothes he is wearing, his jewelry, accessories, hair, etc. At a given moment the A's turn their backs, on cue, and the B's change some detail of their appearance. They may put a wrist watch on the other arm, remove an earring or a pin, button or unbutton a jacket, etc. At a second cue from the leader, the A's will turn back to face their partners. They are allowed one minute to determine what change the B's have made.

8. To prepare for this game some homework is required of the leader. He will cut out pictures of very familiar objects from magazine advertisements. These he will mount on colored construction paper. He will need about thirty of these for a class of twenty. Again the work will be done in pairs, but only five pairs will work at a time. Partner A will be given six pictures which he will arrange on the floor in two rows of three each, forming a rectangle. He will ask his B partner to examine carefully the pictures and their positions in the pattern. Partner B will then turn around, eyes closed, while A changes the position of one or two pictures in the arrangement. Partner B will then be asked to look once more at the pictures, and, if he feels there has been a change, to move

the pictures so that they will create the original design. The game will then be played in reverse order, with the A's doing the guessing; the other five pairs will then take the five sets of pictures and try the exercise.

9. Partner A opens a gift box, takes out something to wear or use, handles it in such a way that his partner B should be able to identify it. He then hands the article to his B partner who, if he has recognized it, will handle it in a way that will show that he knows what it is. This exercise can only be done successfully by those who recall and use the first *KEY*:   *Make a picture in your mind!*

10. A simple action like opening a door or a window for a specific purpose can be interesting. Again, it is essential for the playing partner to have a definite reason for moving to open the door or the window. It can only be real and convincing to his observing partner if the thought pattern is motivated by a clearly imagined dramatic situation. For example, he may hurry to open the door to welcome a beloved grandson returning from a long trip; or, he may open the door sadly and slowly to enter a hospital room where a dear friend is very ill.

GROUP EXERCISES

The following exercises, with the whole group (or half) participating, need no guessing or follow up discussion. The purpose is solely to give the members varied opportunities for expressing thought and feeling.

1. The scene is a railroad station. Decide why you are there—to meet someone perhaps, to leave town quietly, or to escape. The reason is up to you. Suddenly, you hear an announcement on the P.A. system "No trains in or out of town today. Trouble on the main tracks." How does this affect you? What are your thoughts? React as you would in your specific situation.

2. Stand or sit and lift your right hand into the air, high over
   your head. Try to imagine a situation in which this gesture
   would mean something. Use your hand and arm in such a
   way that you can be seen as a definite character in a
   specific situation. (Examples: One might be reaching for
   something on a high shelf; another may be waving
   goodbye to friends leaving on a plane; someone else could
   be holding on to the cord of a kite.)

3. This exercise is intended to sharpen the sense of hearing as
   well as develop concentration. The leader may tap out a
   rhythmic sequence with a pencil on a hard surface, or by
   merely clapping his hands. He will then ask anyone who
   can to repeat the exact pattern. Example: He may tap
   four quarter notes (1111), a whole note (1---), four
   quarter notes (1111), and finally two half notes (1-1-); or
   he may clap his hands twice over his head, twice behind
   his back and then four times on his knees. Any number of
   the group may offer to repeat the pattern, one at a time.

4. The leader may arrange five or six objects on a tray, place
   the tray, covered, on a table in the center of the room. He
   will then remove the cover, and ask the participants (all or
   half the group) to line up and walk slowly past the tray,
   observing the objects very carefully. They will return to
   their seats and try to write down on paper provided them,
   the list of objects they have seen.

5. This is another exercise for sharpening mental imagery,
   which can be done by all or half the group at one time.
   They may imagine themselves coming out into a garden
   and seeing an unusually beautiful butterfly, fluttering
   from one shrub or bush to the next. Each will try to
   approach it quietly, carefully. Finally, he will stretch out
   an arm to let the butterfly move on to his wrist and then
   slowly walk up to his shoulder. After a moment, it will fly
   away and disappear. Coaxing a squirrel to eat from one's

hand or feeding fish in a pond can serve the same purpose.

6. What we call the "Refrigerator Game" is a team effort and a great deal of fun. If the class is not too large, it can involve the whole group, using perhaps ten on each team. The two teams stand (or sit) in a long line, one behind the other. The first in each line imagines he has a refrigerator in front of him. These two are secretly told by the leader what they are to take from the refrigerator (a bottle of coca cola, a piece of watermelon, a leg of chicken, a cup of pudding with a spoon, anything edible or potable). The other nine, in each line, turn their backs as the first one goes to get his article from the refrigerator. He returns and taps number two in line on the shoulder. Number two turns and watches carefully what number one does with his food (or drink). He tries to guess what it is. When he feels sure, he takes it, taps number three on the shoulder. Number three, turns and watches number two eat or drink in pantomime trying to picture what he has in his hand. The same action occurs all the way down the line until the last one on the team has received the food. He tells his team what he thinks he has received. Usually he discovers, much to his amusement, that the article, in passing through ten pairs of hands, has become something entirely different. Should the participants on either team be observant enough, and sufficiently accurate in their pantomime to get the article to the end of the line in its original shape, they have obviously won the match. There are many ways this kind of game can be varied and the activity is always challenging and enjoyable.

Although these warm-ups require only a few minutes and may seem more like party games than activities designed to further growth and change, they do provide many benefits.

Some older people may have had a long and uncomfortable trip to reach the creative drama class; some are not feeling in perfect shape physically; others may have received some disquieting news in the morning mail. They may not be ready to involve themselves immediately in complex improvisations. They need some light, pleasant stimulus to help them forget their personal problems and open their minds and hearts to one another. These relatively simple exercises, and others like them, serve that purpose remarkably well.

Some of the exercises suggested in the next chapter for less mobile seniors may also be adapted for use as warm-ups and ice-breakers.

9

Working With Less Mobile Seniors

Many leaders have approached me recently with requests for guidance in working with seniors who are living in nursing homes or rehabilitation centers. Such institutions do present special problems. Many of these residents are partially immobilized; some are very depressed and some are openly hostile and prey to destructive self-pity. If we, as leaders, are to give genuine help to this group, we must look closely at every individual, analyzing his background, his physical problems and the incidents or relationships which have caused him to become so lonely, so empty, so fragile. As we study and learn, we can, perhaps, compassionately identify with him and adapt our program to fill his needs more appropriately.

As potential leaders we must recognize this kind of situation and seek ways in which we can gradually help these people to once more become individuals, comfortable with their own very special differences. We will try to assist them to function more adequately by realizing their own potentials to create and imagine to the fullest possible extent, no matter what their condition. This implies seeking out every known method to develop awareness, sensitivity and responsiveness, thus increasing their ability to interact with others.

If we are honest, we will recognize the fact that there are certain aspects of the human person which function less effectively as he grows older. In the case of institutionalized seniors with limited mobility, this condition is much more advanced and severe. Although they themselves often recognize this change, or what some may call "deterioration," they often tend to accept it as inevitable and final. While no easy solutions are available, and one cannot expect dramatic reversals and consistent results with every individual, it would be defeatist to passively accept the situation as inevitable. The wise leader should openly and honestly analyze and discuss these problems. He can explain how a fresh point of view, new interests and experiences can offer revitalization, refreshment and a partial solution to some of the difficulties. And, here, the sessions devoted to creative drama exercises can be put at the top of the list of remedies. As with other seniors in all six groups, there was a noticeable change even among the less mobile seniors after several weeks. They felt senses quickened, imaginative powers growing and their ability to identify with others steadily extended. As the good feeling increased, the less mobile seniors seemed to arrive at a sensitive understanding of their problems and were more readily able to take a fresh look at themselves as individuals. This should encourage all leaders to review their goals and objectives, and set about adapting materials which can be used effectively.

EXERCISES

The following exercises are divided into four sections.

1. For these, the leader will collect some familiar articles, perhaps a clothes pin, a flower holder, bracelet, shell, scissors, gold chain, pencil, sunglasses, adhesive tape, light bulb, etc. These may be used in various ways to develop powers of observation and further concentration and to stimulate the imagination.

   A. Place one object, unseen by the rest, in the hands of one individual; he will hold it behind his back. He will describe the shape, size, texture, weight, or any other identifying characteristics. As soon as someone else thinks he can name it, he raises his hand and speaks out. If it is not right another person may venture a guess. The person who makes the correct guess has a chance to hold another object behind him, and describe it for the rest to guess. This kind game can be tried with a half dozen articles; it can continue as long as interest is keen.

B. About ten articles are placed on a low table or on the floor where they can be seen easily by everyone. All should be asked to look carefully at the number of articles present as well as their arrangement on the table. The leader then suggests: "Turn and close eyes." While the participants are faced away from the table, the leader either removes one or two articles, changes the positions of several or changes the condition of one or two (Example: Open a locket, close a safety pin, open scissors.) On cue, the members re-examine the table to discover what change has been made. They may write down their answers on paper provided or they may simply raise their hands if they want to guess. The members may do this without the leader. They may be divided into four groups of five. One in the group will make the change in the arrangement and the others will have a chance to guess. The first to guess correctly may make the next change.

C. The articles are once again arranged on a tray or table. Two groups of three will be asked to select a pair of articles that seem to be compatible, or have the same characteristics. Another three may choose a pair which seem to be opposites.

Example:

Similar	Opposites
Bracelet and chain (jewelry)	Adhesives and scissors (one cuts/the other holds together)
Nail clippers and scissors (both cut)	Sunglasses and electric bulb (one gives light/the other takes it away)
Thimble, and tape measure (sewing)	

D. A small group of three or four may be asked to take from the objects on the table, several which might be used to tell a story. They go apart, discuss their ideas until time is called (about five minutes is usually enough). They then return to their places and tell their story, all participating. This kind of exercise could be done simultaneously by several groups, if they remember their articles rather than actually removing them from the table.

E. The same plan as that described in D can be used, except that the objective is to let the chosen articles suggest a dramatic story which can be improvised by the group members. To facilitate this playing, a list of places, one of which is to be used as the scene for the drama, may be written on a blackboard.

2. The following exercises are all done with cards showing drawings or pictures of various objects. Some simple and familiar objects can be drawn in pen and ink or cut from magazine advertisements. They must be very clear, and each card should contain only a picture of one article. The following could be used: boat, knife, needle, camera, thimble, shoe, bottle, toothbrush, suitcase, keys, hammer, comb, pill bottle, saw, spade, and so forth.

A. Each person takes a card, face down, and puts it on the floor or table in front of him. On cue he turns it up, examines it, and attempts to associate with it. In a few moments, the leader asks each person, in order, to verbalize about his article. Did it remind him of an incident, something in the past, a person? What were his thoughts as he first looked at the drawing? Only about ten should play this game at once, for it is difficult to make more than ten or fifteen cards.

B. A variation on exercise A has proved to be great fun. The cards are put out together, in a rectangle, on the table or floor. Each person then chooses which he associates with a person. For example, keys might mean St. Peter at the gate; the pill bottle, a hypochondriac neighbor who is always taking pills; the needle or scissors might suggest a famous designer, and so on.

C. Several of the same cards may be selected by groups of three or four. The little team will be asked to pick out cards which seem to suggest characteristics. Some of the articles—like hammer, knife, scissors, etc. might suggest hard, cutting, malicious, unyielding individuals; others may imply soft, tender, calm personalities. Each group will arrange its selected cards and explain the reasons for their choices.

D. The articles can also be used to invent a story or inspire an improvisation to be played by a small group of the more mobile members. (This is similar to the plan suggested in 1-E.)

3. For these exercises, photographs, drawings, or advertisements representing character faces will be collected by the leader and mounted on pieces of cardboard or colored construction paper. Each face should portray some definite mood or strong emotion so that the participants can easily identify with them as people, catch their feelings and imagine their life patterns.

A. Each person takes (or is given) one picture. He looks at

it carefully, studies and analyzes the face to determine what it says about the individual. He will then try to develop some interesting biographical facts about his new "friend" including his possible age, profession, status, background, perhaps even problems which may beset him. After a few minutes, any member who has finished creating his small biography may offer to tell his story. Finally, he shows his picture, and the rest may comment on how closely the photograph resembles the character described. They may add some interesting additional facts about his personality, which they have observed. (It has been most satisfactory to plan only five or six of these at a time.)

B. This exercise works well when it is done in groups of three or four. One or all members of the group may select two or three face pictures, which they find interesting and possible to interrelate in a story. A time limit is set for the small group discussions; ten minutes might be needed. At the end of the period, the groups may tell their original stories. They will show the face pictures which had inspired them and explain how the story had developed.

C. The same idea used in B can provide material for dramatic improvisations, if any group is able to move easily, and wishes to play the story, rather than tell it.

D. All the pictures may now be lined up on a table, face up. Five participants are each asked to concentrate on one picture, keeping his selection a secret. After a few minutes, each one will describe the character of the face he has chosen. The rest will listen carefully, and then try to guess which character face the speaker is describing.

4. The following assignments and games depend upon the spoken word. They require great concentration, imagination, association of ideas and often a fairly

extensive vocabulary. Although such games often become contests when the speed of replying is important, this is *not* suggested for the senior group. Many are disconcerted and uncomfortable when subjected to the stress and competition. If, after a reasonable time span, the answer is not forthcoming, it is advisable, for practical reasons, to pass along to the next person in the circle.

A. For this one, the leader will have made large cards on which he has written nouns such as *Trees, Flowers, Boats, Birds, Fish, Animals,* etc. These will be kept face down on the table. One at a time, the leader will hold up a card and ask for a reply. Example: He holds up the card which says *Fish*, and several answers come immediately, *Trout, Rock, Perch,* etc. If one participant can act as secretary, she might jot down the answers on a blackboard. They very much enjoy seeing how many words they can find that fit each category.

B. Cards containing adjectives will be needed for this one. As the leader holds up a card, he will ask for a word which has the opposite meaning.

Example: *Short* - (tall)   *Cold* - (hot)
         Smooth - (rough)   *Ugly* - (beautiful)
         Sweet - (sour)   *Mean* - (kind, pleasant)
         Peaceful - (warlike) *Big* - (small)

C. To play this game one needs only to be able to spell, listen carefully, think and recall. It is called The Alphabet Game. One participant, or the leader, starts with a word beginning with A. The next in the circle must say a word beginning with B; the next thinks of a C word and so it goes around the circle until the letter Z has been used. One can go twice through the alphabet, and abide by the rule that no word may be used a second time. Anyone who cannot think of a word in about thirty seconds just says "pass" and the next one provides it.

D. An adaptation of the game described in C is starting with any word at all and asking the next person to think of a word beginning with the last letter of the word given. Example: The first says "Apple," the second must say a word beginning with E. The word "End" will do. The next in the circle will give a word using the D, maybe "Dog." This can go on as long as there is interest in the game.

E. The last of these word games is great fun, but is far more demanding than the others. It is recommended only for those groups who have already been working together with dialogue exercises and would therefore feel comfortable enough to participate. A small group of four or five is seated together. The leader sets the imagined scene, as well as their supposed relationship to one another. For example, the leader may say, "You are a group of friends, gathered together around the fireplace in a mountain cabin in Maine, belonging to one of you." Then one member of the group is taken aside and quietly given a single line of dialogue by the leader. For example, he might suggest: "I can't find it!" This line is to be said by the member selected, as he comes in through an imaginary door. Someone, anyone, may respond to the statement, "I can't find it!" They will try to keep the conversation flowing until a logical and possible end to the story is reached. Obviously, the rest of the members are startled when the line is spoken. Most likely someone will ask, "Can't find what?" The answer to this question will give them some key information on which they can build the scene. If the reply comes, "You know, the box I put in the attic," someone is sure to ask what was in it or who could have taken it. Perhaps someone will finally suggest that they call the police. They rise and go to the telephone and thus the scene will end! (This plan is similar to that suggested in Chapter 6. Exercise 3, page 79).

F. A final word game, originating as a party game many years ago, can often be used successfully with a circle of senior participants. It is called "Buzz" and this is the important word to remember, and the key to remaining in the game. Someone is asked to start to count beginning with the number one. The neighbor on his left says two, the next three and so on. Each time the number 7 in any form or any multiple comes up, the player, instead of saying the number, says Buzz, and the next player goes on with the sequential number. Anyone who speaks the number seven, or a multiple thereof, instead of saying Buzz, automatically drops out of the game. Numbers such as 7, 17, 47, are easy to recognize; it is easy to fail, however, on such numbers as 49 and 56. The game can stop at any time. It is best not to go much further than 100 or the products resulting from the use of the twelve table. More complex multiplication or division may be tensing rather than just fun.

The suggestions made in this chapter for ways to work with less mobile seniors will hopefully provide hints and tips for many approaches to the problem. Although none of the exercises given are related to the sense of hearing, sharpening listening powers can be interesting and helpful. The leader, or one of the members, may beat out a rhythm with cymbals, a small drum or tambourine, or even an empty coffee can with a plastic top will serve the purpose. As they listen, a member who has caught the rhythm may ask for the instrument, repeat the measure, and then add another measure to the original pattern. Still a third or fourth may join the game, if there are those present who can follow more complex drum beats. Whatever the activity, our goal is always the same: to involve the whole group in pleasurable concentrating, communicating and growing!

10
Drama With and For Seniors

THE NATIONAL PICTURE

For the past fifteen years, services for the aging have been of concern throughout the western world. The passing of the Older Americans Act by Congress in 1965 testifies to the fact that the subject is of vital importance to this country's lawmakers. The National Council on the Aging, a private, non-profit corporation under government sponsorship, has served since 1950 as the central resource for research, information, and publications relating to older people. Housing, health, retirement planning, continuing education, and creative use of leisure time are all areas in which NCOA is directly concerned. With headquarters in Washington, D.C., NCOA has grown from a two-member staff organization to an agency with one hundred employees and regional offices in most major cities across the country. It is committed to expanding the options and alternatives in the lives of seniors, and has earned its reputation as the leading national volunteer organization in the field of aging, getting together, as members and consultants, the nation's most prominent professionals and lay persons working in this field.

In 1973, a special division of NCOA called the National Center on Arts and Aging was established under the capable leadership of Jacqueline T. Sunderland. This organization has been working tirelessly to activate local and national groups to consider the important role the arts can play in life enrichment for the elderly. Its leaders believe that today's older Americans, thanks to technology, medical progress and increased longevity, experience an abundance of free, unscheduled time. And, as Jung once said, "Man cannot stand a meaningless life." It is to making life meaningful, through finding creative uses for the seniors' new leisure, that this organization is dedicated.

As early as 1969, Dr. Stanley A. Czurles spoke at a seminar at Union College in Schenectady, New York, on "Enlightening Retirement Living Through the Arts." He said in part, "Age does not stop creative growth, its satisfactions and developmental values . . . on the contrary, it frees the individual for the maximum personal involvement. . . . The arts, through creative activities, can help the aging become increasingly enriching selves." Simone de Beauvoir, in *Coming of Age,* expresses a similar philosophy: "There is only one solution if old age is not to be an absurd parody of our former life, and that is to go on pursuing ends that give our existence meaning . . . devotion to individuals, to groups, or to causes, social, political, intellectual or creative work."

By 1976, every state in the union listed either an office of aging, or an agency designated to implement programs growing out of the Older Americans Act. Many of these state offices offer economic or physical assistance to the elderly. Some are deeply involved in health, housing, and transportation programs; some are also concerned with supporting cultural enrichment and human growth activities. Many communities boast of lively senior centers where counseling, health services, social activities, and entertainment are provided. Supplementary enrichment programs are frequently offered by art museums, theatre and mime groups, colleges and universities. These are far too numerous to mention individually. Unfortunately, however, there are some communities where the question of how seniors spend their leisure time, or how empty their social life has become, is still ignored.

Interest *is* increasing in making the "age of retirement" a time for new discoveries, excitement, enriched human relationships and joy. And there are other hopeful signs! Within the past five years, the daily press and other journals have carried features concerning experiences and contributions of the elderly. Special television programs have also been focused on their problems and achievements. The American Association of Retired Persons has been a strong force in stimulating national interest, as has the Gray Panthers, an organization founded by a dynamic senior, Maggie Kuhn.

Heartwarming indeed is the recent recognition of the benefits derived from intergenerational programs, where an opportunity is provided for the young and old, through combining their efforts on a common project, to get to know and understand one another. Jacqueline Sunderland's fine book, *Older Americans and the Arts: A Human Equation* published by the National Council on the Aging in 1976, describes an exciting experiment started by Geraldine Fitzgerald and Brother Jonathan called "The Everyman Project." It is designed to bring together young and old, and through the dynamics of theatre, help them to develop a sense of mutual concern. About twenty young people aged 14-20 and twenty seniors, all over 65 cooperated in an informal improvisation workshop. They used material, like a modernized "King Lear" theme, to study the basic issues which often surface during young-old relationships. They firmly believe that the spontaneity of the young and the wisdom of the old can combine to deepen human understanding.

Another colleague who is having great success with intergenerational projects is Joyce Chambers-Selber, who has just completed work for her Master's degree at the University of Texas. Her thesis consisted of the story, with complete production notes, of a performance of George Latshaw's *Pinnochio* in which the cast was composed of college students and senior citizens. Grace Stanistreet, at Adelphi University on Long

Island, has been successfully using creative drama as a communication medium between children and seniors. Dr. Milton Polsky of Hunter College, New York, director of the Brookdale Drama Project involving seniors, recently conducted a workshop in which grandparents and grandchildren worked together, utilizing various theatre techniques. In 1975, Professor Coleman Jennings, of the University of Texas Theatre Department, initiated an interesting junior-senior program. He cast fifteen black women, over 65, as chorus members in a children's play by Aurand Harris, *Steal Away Home.* The audience of children to which the company played was attentive and enthusiastic. In South Carolina a group of six seniors from a senior citizen club performed on live television and dramatized a series of folk stories and fairy tales for preschool children which they played at libraries and day-care centers. They, too, were enthusiastically received by their young audiences. Their artistic director reports: ". . . they seemed to have emerged from their shells and to have become more interested in the world about them. Their reception has given them fresh feelings of importance in the world."

In Baltimore, in 1977, a small creative drama class of children between the ages of 11 and 14, which I had been conducting at the College of Notre Dame of Maryland, came to me with a delightful idea. They asked if they might create a short play which they could tour to senior centers and retirement homes. They had even selected a name for their company: *The Young Pretenders.* During the first season we played sixteen performances on weekends from March to May. The dozen young people, assisted only by Sister Kathleen Marie, Chairman of the Drama Department, myself, and one or two volunteers, gathered properties, designed costumes, packed and unpacked simple scene units, and carried on a spirited question-and-answer period with the seniors after each performance. Their reputation soon

spread, and before the last weekend, we had received thirty
more requests for performances than we could possibly fill.
The seniors were an enthusiastic audience. The Young Pretenders were deeply gratified as they sensed the joy their
efforts had brought to so many!

OTHER SENIOR PROGRAMS AROUND THE COUNTRY

I am deeply grateful to Joyce Chambers-Selber for the
timely appearance of her thesis! It made its bow shortly
before this book went to press, and I am therefore able, with
her permission, to give my readers the benefit of her thorough
research concerning other senior programs in this country. A
cursory listing here will indicate how broad the scope of
interest in drama for seniors has become. I shall list progams
geographically.

The Eastern States

1. Washington, D.C.: The Living Stage, under the direction
   of Robert Alexander, involves seniors in improvisational
   theatre.
2. Atlanta, Georgia: The Georgia Gerontological Society of
   Atlanta, thanks to a small grant, was able to engage a
   drama teacher to form a creative drama workshop for the
   aging. The twelve members of the group formulated a
   drama, *Yesterday's Children,* which is concerned with
   problems the aging face with regard to health, recreation,
   income and housing. They have given performances to
   various audiences and have been very well received.
3. Baltimore County, Maryland: Paul Boxell directs the
   Autumn Players, an over-sixty drama group at Catonsville Community College.
4. Olney, Maryland: Morris Engel, a senior citizen equity
   actor, has started interesting drama workshops for seniors.
5. Detroit, Michigan: Shirley Harbin of the Detroit Recrea-

tion Department and the Theatre Council, coordinates programs for seniors and has compiled an interesting handbook, entitled *Dramatic Activities for the Elderly.*

6. New York, N.Y.: Paula Gray, who surveyed dramatic programs in the New York area in her dissertation study at Columbia University, has published a very useful book on the subject, *Plays for the Elderly.* Dr. Gray is director of activities at the Jewish Home and Hospital for the Aged in New York.

7. White Plains, New York: Ruth Tate has been directing a group of seniors in improvisations and scenes from plays. They have frequently won awards at local community theatre tournaments.

8. Altoona, Pennsylvania: Roger Cornish, having been commissioned by Pennsylvania State University to write some plays for senior actors, established a creative drama workshop in order to understand better the elderly and their needs. This group formed an improvisational company and toured their works to senior centers. After this enlightening experiment, Mr. Cornish, with John Orlock, wrote six plays, published under the title, *Short Plays for the Long Living.*

9. Ambler, Pennsylvania: The Ambler Area Arts Alliance has been sponsoring a new project called Third Age Theatre. It is under the direction of William A. Bauman, David A. France and Rothe G. Freedman. The executive director is Lynne W. Kula. The project is described in the brochure as ". . . a free comprehensive dramatic arts program designed especially for active persons aged 55 and older. Its programs include: a dramatic arts workshop, theatre parties, theatrical productions presented for various community organizations." Since its inception, the group has jointly created several one-act plays, based largely on life experiences. These performances have been successfully

presented at national conferences and toured throughout the area near Ambler.

The Central States

1. Chicago, Illinois: Members of the Free Street Theatre of Chicago, under the direction of Patrick Henry, eager to learn about experiences and needs of older people, set up a creative drama workshop dealing with story-telling. From this project grew the Free Street Theatre Two, composed of twelve seniors. They have traveled, with a van which serves as a stage, to twenty states, communicating the problems of aging through the plays which they perform.

2. Evanston, Illinois: Anne Thurman, Professor of Drama, Northwestern University in Evanston, Illinois, conducts workshops in creative drama and improvisation for those who work with seniors.

3. St. Paul, Minnesota: Bonnie Morris directs an improvisational group called Senior Stars. They present stories shaped from their own experiences and play before seniors, college students and high school groups.

4. Austin, Texas: The Texas Commission on Arts and Humanities awarded a grant to the Austin Repertory Theatre to expand their existing programs to serve additional senior centers and to train leaders to work with seniors in creative drama. This program, called Act Your Age, is expected to serve as a state-wide model.

5. Austin, Texas: There is also a performing company of Black seniors from Salina Recreation Center which grew out of a creative dramatics program in 1977. In 1979, Pat Fisk directed the group in assigning, constructing and performing a puppet play which they adapted from a Bible story. Once referred to as the Salina Players, they are now known as the Salina Celebrities.

6. Houston, Texas: An interesting program called Outreach introduces creative drama to seniors.

7. Madison, Wisconsin: The Civic Repertory Theatre moved their activities to a retirement center. Their objective is to develop a cross-generational exchange and senior improvisation and mime groups.

The Western States

1. Youngstown, Arizona: Dian Rees Evans Shaw, a senior citizen herself, and for many years director of the Cain Park Theatre in Cleveland, has developed an active producing group of seniors and has been presenting plays with them for sixteen years.
2. Salt Lake City, Utah: Ginger Perkins of the Utah Endowment for the Humanities and Roberta Walters of Salt Lake Arts Center have set up drama programs at senior centers throughout the Salt Lake City area.
3. Washington State: Under the leadership of Associate Professor Susan Pearson, some of the University of Washington's graduate students are deeply involved with researching and developing dramatic activities for seniors.

These are only a few of the many dramatic arts programs that are growing in number every day, throughout the country. Although the mention here is limited, in relation to the total picture, and many worthy of listing have probably been unintentionally omitted, the above will serve to point out the rapid expansion of this kind of service, and to convince any "doubting Thomases" that it is answering a real need.

The positive results of these workshops and performances with and for seniors has moved the American Theatre Association to form the Senior Adult Theatre Program (SAT) under the chairmanship of Dr. C. Robert Kase, Professor Emeritus, University of Delaware. This project aims to encourage the initiation of all kinds of theatre experiences with and for seniors. This includes improvisational theatre, performances of plays in traditional style, readers' theatre, workshops in directing, playwriting, etc., attendance at professional theatre performances, and participating in school, college and community theatres. Dr. Kase writes: ". . . it is important to the development of the SAT program that you keep the committee informed concerning your SAT activities." Please send such information to C. Robert Kase, Canterbury Tower, 3501 Bayshore Boulevard, Tampa, Florida 33609. Ms. Patricia Sawyer (25 Welwyn Way, Rockville, MD 20850), who serves on the SAT Committee, is the liaison officer for this committee with the national office of the American Theatre Association in Washington. She has been instrumental in preparing the SAT handbook and guide soon to be published by the Pennsylvania State University Press. This volume will give a detailed account of senior programs through the country.

This past year, encouraged by the work of the SAT project, the Children's Theatre Association, a division of ATA, has organized a separate committee under the chairmanship of Professor Susan Pearson of the University of Washington, in Seattle. This group, called the CTAA Committee for Senior Adult Theatre is especially interested in promoting intergenerational theatre. It is gathering information concerning ways to adapt children's creative drama techniques for use with seniors, the success of seniors performing for children, and vice-versa, and the feasibility of using casts composed of seniors and juniors. These and other related matters were discussed by committee members at the annual convention of the American Theatre Association, held in New York City in August 1979. In addition to the chairman the committee includes: Dr. Joseph J. Bellinghiere, San Diego State University; Sister Xavier Coens, Clark College; Naomi Fell, Cleveland, Ohio; Susan Haas, University of Michigan; Don Laffoon, Laguna Beach California; Claire Michaels, Geriadrama Workshops, Jackson Heights, N.Y.; Milton Polsky, Hunter College, N.Y.; Anne Thurman, Northwestern University,

Evanston, Illinois; Naida Weisberg, Providence, Rhode Island, and myself.

Several members of this committee and one or two others engaged in successful work with seniors have, at the author's invitation, sent more detailed information concerning their projects. I am honored to include it in this volume.

1. At Hunter College's Center for Lifelong Learning, Dr. Milton Polsky has designed and directed the highly successful Brookdale Drama Project for Senior Adults. He is the co-producer of the widely-acclaimed video-documentary, *The Brookdale Drama Project: Creative Drama in Action.* His book, *Creative Drama in Later Life,* will be published by Baker's Plays. He has also contributed to Springer's forthcoming book, *Old Age on the New Scene.* Polsky says in the brochure about his creative drama workshop, "Let yourself go! Relax in a creative atmosphere where everyone's imagination is encouraged. In a warm, supportive setting, you will have opportunities to improvise situations and scenes from your past experiences, to stretch your body awareness through easy creative movement, and to enact and reflect on important here-and-now concerns through creative games and role-playing." He also holds playreading workshops where modern playwrights are studied, scenes played, and the thematic material of the plays examined in relation to the lives of the participants.

2. Claire Michaels, originator of the "Geriadrama" workshops in Jackson Heights, New York, has had remarkable success with her training sessions for the study of what she calls "actualization techniques for the older person." Ms. Michaels is a drama therapist, a graduate of New York University in educational theatre and therapeutic recreation and a performing artist as well as a founding member of New York's Circle-in-the-Square Theatre. She has ingeniously combined her professional training in psycho-drama

and socio-drama techniques with the gerontological, recreational and arts fields to create Geriadrama.[1] She describes her project very clearly: "Geriadrama is a technique of informal creative dramatics and spontaneity training combined with other art forms, designed to provide older persons with the opportunity to act and 'try out' processes of the imagination, ventilate their emotions and evoke memory recall. It is serious playacting that gives pleasure, releases tensions, sparks positive energy, improves concentration and raises self-esteem. Through the uses of music, movement, spoken and written language and memorabilia, the creative potential is stimulated, leading to a more productive life." She has had unusual success with her methods in settings as varied as senior centers, rehabilitative environments, hospitals and recreation centers. She has been invited to conduct training workshops in many parts of this country and Canada.

3. Susan Haas is research assistant at the Institute of Gerontology at the University of Michigan.[2] She has been developing curriculum materials for introducing gerontological content to journalism courses. She is also interested in ". . . the development of a book, or at least some source materials, that would focus on dramatic activities and experiences with the elderly." She is available to assist others with background material on aging.

4. Dr. Joseph J. Bellinghiere has received a grant from the California Department of Health to investigate the use of drama with the senior adult. He has recently given a lecture/workshop on "Creative Drama and the Gerontologist" at the Western Gerontological Convention in San Francisco and is working on a resource book to be called *Creative Drama and the Senior Adult.*

[1]Claire Michaels 1978—all rights reserved.

[2]For detailed information about The Institute of Gerontology, see page 130.

5. Don Laffoon has had international experience in all phases of theatre. He and his wife are at present using dramatic techniques to bring a new self-awareness to seniors. His pilot project, including seven senior groups, has been sponsored by the South Coast Repertory Theatre in California. He states his purpose this way: ". . . to help the older citizens develop better communication among themselves and with the Community—to improve their self-image and tap their individual creativity." At the close of this pilot project Laffoon hopes to analyze his research and set down some workable principles which will apply to all uses of drama with and for seniors.

6. Joyce Chambers-Selber, to whose M.A. thesis I am indebted for much of the historical data in this chapter, deserves special mention here because of her unique work under the tutelage of Dr. Coleman Jennings at the University of Texas in Austin. In 1976 she became involved in a creative drama program at several senior centers, initiated by Jo Lynn Hoffman and Lynn Wilford, graduate students in Dr. Jennings' Theatre for Youth project. At present writing, the program has been enlarged to include a total of six centers and Beryl Knifton has joined Ms. Chambers-Selber in its direction.

   Her thesis project, the production of the George Latshaw *Pinnochio* script, was designed as "an artistic and social awareness experiment with senior citizens performing for children." Ms. Chambers-Selber says that she made the choice "because of its emphasis on the growth process throughout life." The experiment, when put into practice, became an immediate success. Her cast included people between the ages of nineteen and eighty, and they gave eight performances in all, several of which were given for audiences of elementary school children.

7. From the Institute of Gerontology, co-sponsored by the University of Michigan and Wayne State University, come

the following comments on their current program. We are indebted to Lila Green, Project Coordinator in Continuing Education, for this detailed report. The co-directors of the Institute of Gerontology are Harold R. Johnson and Charles J. Parrish. For the past three years Ms. Green has planned these seminars, entitled "Drama and Literature Programs for the Elderly."

The brochure for the 1979 seminar begins with this statement: "Old age can be a time for continued growth and development, for new roles and creative endeavors, for continuing life satisfaction." It goes on to describe the program's plan and purpose: "The seminar was designed to present a wide cross-section of programs that are taking place in drama as well as 'how-to' workshops. . . . Literature was incorporated into the program because much of the material used in dramatic activities originated from reminiscences, oral history, poetry, memoirs, etc. . . . The participants ranged from activity directors, program co-ordinators, senior center administrators and volunteers, to physicians and social workers. . . . Evaluations reflected high enthusiasm for the content and the wide range of presentations. . . . The Michigan Council for the Arts helped support the seminar in 1978." The seminar meetings were held on three consecutive days, at all-day sessions, July 9, 10, 11, 1979. Some of the subject titles were provocative and challenging, for example: 1) Techniques of Oral History, 2) Clown Ministry, 3) Autobiography Writing, 4) Making Poems a Group Adventure, 5) The Oldsters' Mime Company, 6) Using Readers' Theatre with Oldsters.

8. Naida Weisberg, the founder and president of an exciting project in Rhode Island, describes her unique program this way: 'Improvise! Inc.,' is a non-profit organization of creative drama specialists located in Providence, Rhode Island. When the local State Council on the Arts, which helps to subsidize many of our in-school programs, estab-

lished a Community Arts division a couple of years ago, monies for Arts and Aging were included. This subsidy comes from the Rhode Island Department of Elderly Affairs which receives its funding from the federal government via the Older Americans Act.

The various residential homes for seniors and day care centers are kept informed about the availability of artists who generally work with their groups once a week for 10-12 sessions; the programs are often renewed if the experience has been mutually satisfying. In most cases, the Arts Council pays half the artist's fee and the sponsoring agency the other half. However, when the sponsor is fundless, the council will sometimes assume the entire cost. One requirement of the artist and the sponsoring agency is a written evaluation at the project's end which covers goals and actual outcomes, the degree of participant involvement, overall impact, successes and failures, problems, changes noted, etc.

Since the beginning of Arts and Aging, we have conducted programs in many different ethnic settings: Irish, Black, Jewish, Italian and 'mixed.' The groups have varied in number from eight to twenty-five. But we are also working with activities directors of nursing homes who are making plans to take our eight-week course after the first of the year. Approximately 25 women and one man will come to a designated nursing home—or homes—one morning a week for the duration of the course and we will demonstrate our approach with some of the patients at each session for part of the time. As one activities director commented, 'What you people do really fits in with our re-motivation techniques.'

Good feelings of satisfaction on the part of both leader and seniors are mutual. When you hear such statements as 'I haven't had so much fun since I was a kid!' and 'Is this therapeutic or something? My vocal chords are all relaxed!', you know you're doing important work!

Three books that are inspirational for the creative drama teacher of seniors are: *What's Inside You, It Shines Out Of You* by Mark Kaminsky, Horizon, 1977; *Therapeutic Dance/Movement, Expressive Activities for Older Adults* by Erna Caplow-Lindner, Human Sciences Press, 1979; and *I Never Told Anybody, Teaching Poetry Writing in a Nursing Home,* Random House, 1977.''

9. ''SPICE'' is an intergenerational drama pilot workshop designed and led by Professor Susan Pearson of the University of Washington School of Drama in Seattle. It brings together equal numbers of senior adults and elementary students to do creative drama for an hour each week. Activities are designed to make participants aware of their own expressive abilities and to enhance self-confidence and self-esteem. The seniors meet each week for a half-hour before the young people arrive to warm up and help the leader plan final details of the session. The seniors, in effect, become a teaching team assisting the group leader. Subject matter for each session grows out of the interests of group members, and an emphasis is placed on letting seniors and children learn what they have in common as well as the differences they experience. Past topics have included: favorite leisure activities, re-enacting incidents from ''first holidays you can remember,'' dreams, sibling and parent squabbles, and finding skills which old and young can teach each other. Fairy tales have also been very popular stimuli for drama with both age groups. The high point for many of the seniors has been enjoying the energy and spontaneity of the children. The children, usually selected by teachers from the second and third grade classes, particularly enjoy the one-to-one contact with adults which their regular school program cannot provide.

The title of the program comes from its sponsoring organization: ''School Programs Involving our Community's Elderly.'' SPICE has as its purpose promoting independent living and preventing isolation by providing food, health care, and social and recreational services for senior citizens. Its centers are located in Seattle Public Schools, so SPICE also provides seniors with the opportunity to make a real contribution to the education of children. Many SPICE members tutor, teach workshops, and assist school nurses and staff members. The drama program increases the intergenerational contact which SPICE has set as another of its goals. The assumption underlying the drama workshop is that, by bringing children into contact with seniors who are experiencing life satisfaction, some of the negative stereotypes of aging can be prevented.

Although this survey of some of the exciting drama programs in progress across the country is necessarily brief and incomplete, it is my fervent hope that it may serve two purposes:

1) to deepen the growing conviction that seniors can be a rich resource rather than a difficult problem;
2) to persuade cultural, social, and educational institutions that they must assume leadership in separating the myths from facts concerning aging and take firm steps to provide seniors with opportunities for growth and enrichment, so that they may enjoy the full human experience.

11
In Conclusion

This final chapter must be a kind of remembering, a kind of personal summing up. It is also a witnessing to an exciting discovery which has brought immeasurable joy and satisfaction to my own "senior" years.

My earliest experiments in the use of creative drama were born out of necessity, when at the age of sixteen, I had my first job as junior counselor at a girls' summer camp in New Hampshire. During the second week, early in July, the director, Miss Mary Elcock, called me into her office. She explained her anxiety over a rash of homesickness among the nine-to-eleven-year-olds. And then came a shocking directive: "My dear Isabel, you simply *must* find a way to cure this dreadful ailment. Just four years ago, your first at camp, you suffered from the same disease, remember? And you found the way, in a few weeks, to become the happiest, most contributive member of my Camp Asquam family. Now it's your turn to share your secret with those who need you."

I swallowed hard; for a time I couldn't speak. When I could find my voice, I was tempted simply to refuse the assignment; it seemed an impossible task. Then, quite suddenly, memories came flooding back. I saw clearly that moment, four years ago, to which Miss Elcock had referred, that moment when I had lost my way, and then found it. I accepted the assignment.

How well I recall my heartaches, the flood of tears which

134

soaked my pillow every night of my first week at camp; I tried so hard to smother those giveaway sounds of homesickness. I also remembered the one statement, made by that dear lady, on our first Sunday night, at her Evensong talk. I can hear it as though it were yesterday. It had turned everything around for me. "There are a few of you," she said sadly, "whose thoughts of self are making you blind and deaf to the beauty all around you. Your homesickness keeps you from seeing the deep blue of our beautiful lake, from hearing the wind in the birches and the plaintive song of the loons. I am distressed about what you are missing, and sorry for the parents who have made real sacrifices to give you this wonderful opportunity."

My heart ached more than ever as I listened to her words. I felt chastened and guilty. I knew those words were meant for me. I turned my face away in the twilight shadows lest it reveal my sad plight. Her voice continued: "Let us promise each other that beginning tonight, we're going to change! I ask you, just for one day, to follow my advice, my prescription for happiness." As she paused, I almost held my breath for fear of missing a single word. "Beginning tomorrow morning, when you awaken, try to think every moment of something you can do to give one of your tent-mates pleasure. Don't let a single thought of what *you* want, or need, cross your mind all day. By evening, you will be happy children, I promise." I was glad the closing hymn was a familiar one; even though I spoke the words automatically no sound came; my heart and mind were elsewhere. I was desperately grasping at straws, but I knew that even though I was far from convinced, I must give the "prescription" a try.

You can guess the end of the tale! The promised miracle occurred. Each day I grew happier, more aware of the goodness and beauty around me. The secret—so simple to say and so hard to do—was *forget self*! Forget self-pity, self-pride, self-hate! As I recalled the transformation I had experienced,

I knew at once what I must do for the homesick children.

It was in the process of seeking ways to help these little ones to stop feeling sorry for themselves, that I discovered, what is known today a half-century later, as *creative drama.* In our free time, we played pretend games, improvised little scenes from life experiences or stories. As the destructive self thoughts were replaced by thoughts and feelings of other individuals, a catharsis, the release and cleansing of destructive emotions originally described by Aristotle, took place. A refreshment, a renewal, a sense of well-being and enthusiastic interaction developed in a remarkably short time.

From that precious moment on, for half a century, I have been trying to discover new ways to use this simple but powerful technique to offer children, young people, and teachers refreshing and enriching experiences to further their self-fulfillment. And now, today, the final chapter is being written as I watch some of our seniors' drawn faces relax, dull eyes regain a sparkle, and smiles replace grim frowns! Positive change has been evident in almost all of the hundred and fifty seniors we have reached in our program.

Although we can make no claim to scientific measurement of individual growth, we did have some very encouraging comments from a visitng psychologist who observed and noted change during the first two experiments conducted in 1976. The results of his· study and that of Sister Timothy Prokes, theologian and psychologist at the College of Notre Dame of Maryland, should be worth notice here. Comments from both bear out my conviction that group work in creative drama has enormous potential for motivating awareness, imagination and warm human relationships.

Dr. William R. Mueller, our first visiting psychologist, says, in part: "The success of the 'Dynamic Living in Retirement' project, I know at first hand, through attending some of the meetings and talking with many of the participants. Time after time they spoke of the course as an event which brought them new hope, new energy, new confidence and new life.''

A summary of the questionnaire given at the end of the course, follows:

	Percentage of Change		
Questions	*No change*	*Some change*	*Much change*
Are you more content and comfortable with yourself?	5%	40%	55%
Has your interest in helping friends and neighbors changed?	5%	40%	55%
Do you find it easier to make decisions?	10%	35%	55%
Are you more aware of sounds, sights, colors?	5%	35%	60%
Has there been improvement in the way you feel physically?	10%	30%	60%
Are you expressing thoughts and feelings more easily?	5%	25%	70%
Are you getting new ideas, finding new ways to solve problems?	10%	20%	70%

The other three questions were the essay type and concerned what they liked most about the course, how they would like to see the format changed, and what kind of qualifications they considered essential for successful leaders. Over ninety percent wanted no change in the format; several suggested that it should go on ''forever''; others wanted to enroll in a post-graduate course. In discussing leadership qualities, those mentioned most frequently were warmth, friendliness, enthusiasm, patience, caring for others, human understanding, knowledge of and proficiency in drama, faith and a positive philosophy.

Because this book is designed to help future leaders in their work with seniors and because Dr. Mueller's final statements indicate what a vital part the leader's philosophy plays in his success, I feel inclined, if a little embarrassed, to include some of his comments. I apologize for their personal implications and hope that my immodesty in relating them will be forgiven:

"What made for the success? The answer is easy—the leadership. How Mrs. Burger made for the success is a more complex matter. She provided inspiration and an incredible ebullience manifesting itself in a tremendous caring for the participants. She was shepherdess of the flock, mother of the tribe. She is, however, more than a personality. She is a skilled teacher. She framed the course beautifully by means of lectures at the first and last meetings. Her first lecture was a spirited call for change in the presumed attitudes of many senior citizens—largely a change from 'poor me' to 'let's open our eyes to what our present world offers.' She urged both a looking out and a dropping of exclusive concern for self. And she explained clearly how creative drama induces a self-forgetfulness and helps an individual to understand and relate to other people. The group was attentive, responsive, appreciative. In her last lecture, Mrs. Burger went back to her first; she spoke of the participants' progress and urged that the end of the course was not a termination but a commencement, one which marks the beginning of a continuation of what had been experienced and learned. She showed herself to be an evangelist and a therapist. 'Magic' just may be the best word to describe the ten-week experience. My effort at description has enjoyed only a partial success. I am not sure that I care very much *how* what happened happened; *that* it happened is a matter about which I care a great deal!"

Sister M. Timothy Prokes, Theology Professor at the College of Notre Dame, added some interesting comments in her evaluation of the third "Dynamic Living in Retirement" course with seniors and the first program for the training of leaders from senior centers. This took place from February to April 1978. She says, in part:

"Without doubt the seminar was an outstanding success. This was evidenced by the response of the trainees as well as the seniors. The sessions are intended to make those who are aging forget their self-preoccupation, live into the real life situations experienced by others, and express their interpretations in spontaneous ways. . . . During the ten weeks, the process helped people to imagine life situations, to think the thoughts of persons involved in such situations, and then to let those thoughts be expressed in body action. . . . By the end of the program, several persons, quite at ease, are able to plan a simple scenario, in which they not only pantomime the appropriate actions but also create spontaneous dialogue. There is no attempt to memorize lines or create a theatre piece. The idea is to elicit from people their capacity to find a bigger world beyond their worries, to identify with others' experiences and to respond genuinely. . . . One of the outstanding traits of the seminar was atmosphere. Genuine care for every person was a hallmark. . . . It was contagious and inspired similar attitudes in the seniors and the trainees. One trainee remarked: 'The atmosphere of warmth and sincerity provided an ease of interaction which added so much to the learning experience. This is a part often overlooked, making this seminar rise above all others I have attended.' "

Sister Timothy went on to examine the results of the questionnaire which included those questions which we had used before. She was very much impressed with the positive replies given by most of the participants.

"In general, the figures show a remarkable effect upon the

seniors . . . and witnessing this has had a great deal to do with the success of the program for the trainees. Some of the joy and ease in the seniors is evident in a videotape, prepared to explain the program.[1] At the beginning and end of this tape, seniors are involved in small scenes, spontaneously lived out before the cameras. Moreover, at one point in the videotape, they tell Mrs. Joyce Di Rienzi,[2] personally, how they grew through their programs with Mrs. Burger, utilizing her techniques and imbibing her philosophy. . . . As official evaluator and visiting scholar, I was impressed with the program and its intensity. The grant, provided by The Maryland Committee for the Humanities, with matching funds from The College of Notre Dame of Maryland, was worth every dollar, many times over.''

There is great joy and satisfaction in every re-reading of the many comments on letters and cards received from our seniors. Some of them I feel compelled to share with my readers, because they express sincerely the depth and breadth of the impact of the ''Dynamic Living'' experiment. A few follow here:

"I've begun to discover myself, thanks to you. I am trying new things and thinking so much better on my feet.''

"I've loved the openness of the whole group and the acceptance of one another.''

"I have enjoyed every minute of being together; there was such a beautiful feeling of congeniality.''

"You make us all feel so good and so happy.''

---

[1]This videotape was planned, written and technically created by ten members of the first senior group, with the assistance of Sister Sharon, director of communications at the college. They wanted to tell their story!

[2]Joyce Di Rienzi, acted as the project director for our first experiments and consolidated all the arrangements with the Maryland Committee for the Humanities, and the College of Notre Dame.

"Creative drama really lifts the spirit; I'm ready to enroll in a post-graduate course."

"It was wonderful to meet so many other people and see them gradually shedding their inhibitions and self-consciousness."

We made the final session of the senior group always a "pot luck luncheon." And it was just what the word implied. With the college's help and Joyce Di Rienzi's leadership, a buffet table was set up to hold all the delicious contributions, coffee and tea were available, and tables, arranged with flowers and candles, added a truly festive air. We decided to make our own creative arts exhibition, so bookcases and tables were filled with handwork, sculpture, paintings, and needlepoint, made by the participants. We presented the little improvised scenes we had been working with, and everyone was involved. The highlights of the second final party, was a beautiful poem, written and read by a frail, 86 year old, Lucille Wilkinson, whose hobby was writing poetry. She called it "A Happy Interlude" and it described her own feelings about our ten weeks together.

A Happy Interlude

How lovely are the hours so dear, that come from who knows where!

They bring along a wealth of cheer, because someone DID care!

Perhaps a word,—maybe a rhyme, carried us back to another time.

A time when we were young and gay, when sunshine sparkled the way!

These precious hours, so short in time, DYNAMIC as they are,

Will live in memory in our hearts—may be our guiding star.

When skies are threatening, dull and gray, when sunshine seems so far away,

Then memory stirs,—and we can say, "Remember all the fun that day?"

As my staff and I exchanged thoughts in our own post-project critique, we tried to determine what special approaches, techniques, behavior patterns, or materials were most contributive to the success we enjoyed. Several things came immediately to mind.

1. The importance of creating a warm, accepting climate, providing love, caring and individual attention, should lead the list. Only in this kind of atmosphere could genuine relaxation take place; only in this freedom from tension and openness can creativity occur.

2. The second and most profound influence came from a completely accidental move on my part. Now that I recognize its power, I shall always include the practice. At the very first meeting, I mentioned during the coffee break that I had found certain wise sayings and quotations so helpful to me, especially in low moments; I had therefore written on the blackboard one that I especially liked and hoped they would enjoy it when we sat down again. I read aloud to them these few words from Sir James Barrie: "Those who bring sunshine into the lives of others, cannot keep it from their own." There was a brisk, delightful discussion about this inspiring thought. Before the session was over we decided to start every class with a favorite quotation. The members offered to help by bringing in some of their own special verses. By the end of the ten weeks we had collected enough words of wisdom to publish a small leaflet for everyone, in mimeograph style.

3. The third supportive effort on the part of the leader is perhaps called a demonstration of faith, a strong, practiced belief in the good and true, in a transcendent God, Creator of all, who loves, forgives, and supports all. Man, especially as he grows older, is still seeking the meaning of life, after

many vicissitudes, disappointments, and much loneliness. If he can be thankful that he still has a chance to renew, learn, listen and serve, and, as a dear friend of mine says, to "seek the will of God for me, today," then life can have a new meaning and new values.

4. One of the most profound effects of the program was the help it gave older people in developing greater awareness, responsiveness and, above all, some commitment. We agreed we must all make a real effort to help them understand the difference between renunciation and resignation; even though there are things which one cannot do physically as one grows older, these renunciations are in the field of action, not of heart and mind. One lives differently but not less; interest and participation in things should not diminish but increase. General MacArthur spoke to this point in 1945 when he said, "You don't get old from living a particular number of years; you get old because you've deserted your ideals. Years wrinkle the skin; renouncing your ideals wrinkles your soul."

In closing, I urge you fervently to look around you, seek out those aging individuals who need renewal, refreshment, caring, guidance, loving. May what I have included in this little book inspire and help you to find your own techniques for accomplishing this most important work. As a final word of encouragement from my mentor, Dr. Paul Tournier, psychiatrist and medical doctor, I inscribe his most illuminating passage on life and age:

"Life is not only expansion, aggression, and domination. It is also love, acceptance, exchange, and communication. . . . one can be successful on into old age through warm-heartedness, readiness to welcome all comers and kindness. . . . You old people, my brethren, come out from behind the doors you have shut upon yourselves and upon your empty inner selves! The world is an exciting place to live in, even when you are no longer playing a dominant part in it. Those are the old folks whom I like to see, their hearts wide open, they are understanding, radiant with love that asks nothing in return, generous, genuine, not envious or jealous. Without having to do or say anything, they impart life, consolation and courage to anyone who goes near them."[3]

We are all growing old; we began the process years and years ago! Let us strive to become one of those beautiful old people whom Dr. Tournier describes and through our own witnessing and growing, let us help those about us to find the way. May God bless your endeavors!

---

[3]Paul Tournier, *Learn to Grow Old,* (New York: Harper & Row, 1972).